Physics and the art of dance

Physics and the

physics and the **art of dance**

art of DANCE

Understanding movement

KENNETH LAWS

PHOTOGRAPHS BY MARTHA SWOPE

OXFORD

UNIVERSITY PRESS

2002

OXFORD
UNIVERSITY PRESS

Oxford   New York
Athens   Auckland   Bangkok   Bogotá   Buenos Aires   Cape Town
Chennai   Dar es Salaam   Delhi   Florence   Hong Kong   Istanbul   Karachi
Kolkata   Kuala Lumpur   Madrid   Melbourne   Mexico City   Mumbai   Nairobi
Paris   São Paulo   Shanghai   Singapore   Taipei   Tokyo   Toronto   Warsaw

and associated companies in
Berlin   Ibadan

Copyright © 2002 by Oxford University Press, Inc.

Published by Oxford University Press, Inc.
198 Madison Avenue, New York, New York 10016

Oxford is a registered trademark of Oxford University Press

Library of Congress Cataloging-in-Publication Data
Laws, Kenneth.
Physics and the art of dance : understanding movement / Kenneth Laws ;
photographs by Martha Swope
p.   cm.
Includes bibliographical references and index.
ISBN 0-19-514482-1
1. Dance—Physiological aspects.   2. Ballet dancing—Physiological aspects.
3. Human mechanics.   4. Biophysics.   I. Title.
QP310.D35 L388 2002
612.'044—dc21   2001035077

1 3 5 7 9 8 6 4 2

Printed in the United States of America
on acid-free paper

Foreword

THE LONGER I teach the more convinced I am of the logic and efficacy of classical ballet technique. While many great pedagogues have codified it in different ways—Bournonville, Legat, Cecchetti, Vaganova, Balanchine among them—the basic principles have remained more or less the same since the latter part of the nineteenth century. This can only be because the exercises work. Good ballet training produces long, supple, strong muscles, awareness and control of the entire body, and the ability to move in many different ways at the request of a choreographer.

The aspect of our work that changes continually, as it should, is our growing use of other disciplines to enhance classical teaching and provide new ways of reaching our students. Kinesiology, psychology, Pilates conditioning, weight-training and the study of anatomy are providing useful tools and raising the bar for each generation of dancers.

But physics? I was more than a little skeptical when Kenneth Laws offered to do a seminar on "Physics and the Art of Partnering" for Pacific Northwest Ballet School's Summer Course students in 1994. We were always eager to explore new ideas so his offer was accepted and twenty young couples were chosen to participate. The day arrived and our students lined up not knowing what to expect but were immediately charmed by Professor Laws's easy manner. At first the exercises and Ken's explanations were deceptively simple but as they went on both the dance sequences and the discussions of physical limitations, possibilities and consequences grew in complexity and fascination. One could see the light dawn on our students' faces as they asked questions and experienced the principles of physics through their own bodies and their interaction with one another. They understood that though we work hard to give the illusion of defying the natural laws, gravity for instance, phyics applies to every movement we make and must be taken into consideration.

For the audience of teachers the greatest benefits of Ken's seminar were the possibilities for injury prevention and the images he gave us, word pictures which proved to be powerful tools in our efforts to reach students' intellects as well as their bodies. When I am asked, as I am very often, to cite the attributes necessary for a career as a classical ballet dancer, I always list "intelligence" first so this has had great appeal for me.

Ken Laws seems to me to be an important ambassador coming to dance from the world of science. He is our interpreter and all his explanations of the physical laws are informed by, and infused with, his great love of dance and dancers. One of the things I prize most about him is that, as passionate as he is about work, he feels, as I do, that technique is only a tool—a beautiful and essential tool but not the ultimate goal. In the end it is the illusion that counts, the character, musicality and intense personal involvement of the dancer that creates a performance.

Francia Russell
Co-director
Pacific Northwest Ballet
July 2001

Preface

THE PHYSICS OF DANCE was published several years after the world of classical ballet turned my life upside down. After teaching college-level physics for more than a dozen years, I was introduced to the beauty of classical ballet *and* discovered that a dance studio is a physics laboratory! There are many intriguing ways of using principles of physics to understand how the human body moves.

Then came that fateful moment when the impetuous me told the rational me, "Hey! Let's write a book about this!" An editor then at Schirmer Books, Maribeth Anderson Payne, went out on a limb and took a chance on the project. Two fine dancers and the premier dance photographer in the country helped make *The Physics of Dance* work.

Ten years later a second book—*Physics, Dance, and the Pas de Deux*—was published by the same publisher and the same editor but with an additional author, Cynthia Harvey, then a principal dancer with American Ballet Theatre. Her contributions included many valuable insights in addition to the credibility that can only come from one so respected in the dance community. We spent many hours struggling to find the common ground that would allow her agile and analytical mind to communicate with my rigorous physicist's mind. I recall trying to convince her that she couldn't move without the floor exerting a force on her, causing

FIGURE P.1. Cynthia Harvey and Robert La Fosse in *Giselle*.

her center of gravity to accelerate. Her answer? "Look! I'm moving!" And she waggled her arms like a bird. I then realized that what *I* meant by "move" referred to the whole body in translational motion; her broader sense of "move" was the common intuitive meaning. This is just one of many lively encounters I had with Cynthia in which our minds came together between the cloud of pure physics reasoning and the ground of common understanding and communication.

I have learned much since that second book was written. A particularly startling revelation has been to see the remarkable ability of even young dancers to understand the pertinent physical principles. The fact that they can *feel* these principles working in their own bodies helps them develop deeper insights than others who only read or hear the ideas described or see them demonstrated. It is also often astonishing to see dancers sense, in some deep analytical part of their minds, how to accommodate to near-impossible challenges. And if dancers have not yet learned to fear science, they are open to the benefits and joys of this analytical level of understanding. Working with dancers has been a privilege and source of great joy to me.

In the eighteen years since *The Physics of Dance* was published, the dance community has become much more open to the science of their art. It is no longer unusual to find dance teachers explaining how forces act on the body from the floor or how to adjust the location of the body's center of gravity in order to accomplish some movement. And it is not unusual to find scientists who enjoy the fact that their science *can* speak usefully to the arts.

This Book Is . . . , It Isn't . . .

This book represents the best from the two earlier books, *The Physics of Dance* and *Physics, Dance, and the Pas de Deux*, illuminated by clearer explanations and enhanced by added features. While many of the ideas, explanations, photographs, and diagrams appeared in one or both of the earlier works, this book includes additional analyzed movements, twenty-five new visuals, and a challenging puzzler for the reader at the beginning of each chapter. Again solo movements are divided into categories for analysis: balance, movements without turns (such as vertical and trav-

FIGURE P.2.
The author "talking physics" with Benjamin Pierce, now principal dancer with San Francisco Ballet, and a young Abi Stafford, now a member of New York City Ballet.

eling jumps), *pirouettes*, and turns in the air. There are three chapters on partnered dance, an expansion beyond the first book but less emphasis than in the second. The effects of body size are discussed for both solo and partnered dance. There is no analysis of ice skating or a specific *pas de deux* (features of the second book) but there are analyses of some additional movements such as the supported lunge. The latter is the subject of the puzzler at the beginning of chapter 6 and of the analysis in appendix K.

A new feature in this book is the anecdotal puzzlers that appear at the beginning of chapters 2–10. They are intended both to reveal briefly the chapter's subject matter and to lead the curious reader into wanting to find the solution to the puzzler, which is buried somewhere within the chapter. Dancers will identify with some of these situations; other readers can imagine them. The "puzzler" idea came from a similar technique used very successfully by Jearl Walker in the fourth edition of *Fundamentals of Physics*, by Halliday, Resnick, and Walker.

This book is intended for a varied audience and so is divided into two parts: the main body and the appendixes. The ten main chapters are intended to be understandable to all who make the effort to think about what they see and feel in dance. Can it be confusing? Of course. But, as Peter Platenius, a psychologist from Queen's University in Canada, has said: "Confusion is the prerequisite for enlightenment." The enlightenment that comes from these analyses can be quite rewarding.

The physicist, the physics student, or just the brave and thoughtful science-minded soul is invited to delve into the appendixes, which describe the basis for many of the claims made in the chapters. For instance, in chapter 3 there is a discussion of the relationship between the height of a jump and the time in the air. The results have profound implications for dancers' sense of tempo and differences in execution of the jumps depending on body size. Appendix A contains the derivation of the equations that lead to those quantitative results.

Although the principles that apply to dance movement are the focus of this book, the intent is not to provide a "how-to" guide that a novice can use to learn dance technique. Many of the movements described and illustrated are those performed by professional dancers and require substantial skilled training. Some of these movements, particularly those involving partners, can be dangerous and should not be attempted without the appropriate training and supervision.

This book does not deal with all forms of dance equitably; it is primarily about the movements of *classical ballet*, not because of a judgment as to the inherent value or worth of that style of dance, but because of the relatively well defined and accepted "vocabulary" of movements and positions. Although there are variations in the style with which balletic movements are carried out by different dancers working with different choreographers, there is fundamentally a "correct" way of performing a *tour jeté*, a *pirouette en dehors*, or a *cabriole en avant*. Analyses of these movements therefore have a generalizable applicability that is potentially useful for any dancer performing any dance movements.

Modern, jazz, or ballroom dance, and even some forms of folk dance, share with ballet many similarities in the types of movements on which these styles are based. Turns on one foot are *pirouettes* whether executed in balletic form with the gesture leg in a *retiré* position or with some other body position called for by the style of the dance form. Jumps, leaps, partnered lifts, balance positions, and essentially any other type of dance movement one can imagine can all be analyzed using the techniques described in this book. Ballet is merely the most convenient vehicle for the analyses since it is the most well defined, constant, and universal style of dance and is the form of dance most familiar to me.

The Artists

Many of the photographs appearing in this book are taken from *The Physics of Dance* and/or *Physics, Dance, and the Pas de Deux*. Two dancers—Lisa de Ribère and Sean Lavery—spent a long and exhausting day in the summer of 1983 performing for the photographer the movements analyzed in *The Physics of Dance*.

Ms. de Ribère is a native of York, Pennsylvania, and received early training at the Central Pennsylvania Youth Ballet and at the school of the Pennsylvania Ballet. After three years at the School of American Ballet she joined George Balanchine's New York City Ballet at the age of sixteen. She danced and toured extensively with

FIGURE P.3. Lisa de Ribère and Sean Lavery, the two dancers who performed movements for the photographs first appearing in *The Physics of Dance* (1984).

that company until 1979, when she joined American Ballet Theatre, where she appeared in numerous principal roles. She toured in 1981 as Alexander Godunov's partner. More recently she has been gaining a broad reputation as a freelance choreographer, setting ballets for companies all over the world.

Sean Lavery is from Harrisburg, Pennsylvania, and also received early training at the Pennsylvania Ballet and the Central Pennsylvania Youth Ballet. After a stint in New York at the Richard Thomas School, he joined the San Francisco Ballet in 1973, then the Frankfurt Opera Ballet in 1975. A year in New York at the School of American Ballet was followed by a long association with the New York City Ballet. After dancing many principal roles with that company, health problems forced him to retire from active dancing. He became ballet master and has also choreographed a number of works.

The subjects for the newer photographs appearing in *Physics, Dance, and the Pas de Deux* are Julie Kent and Benjamin Pierce. Ms. Kent has been a principal dancer with American Ballet Theatre (ABT) since 1993, having joined the company in 1986. In 1986 she was the only American to win a medal at the prestigious Prix de Lausanne International Ballet Competition. She has danced the lead roles at ABT in *Anastasia, La Bayadère, Cinderella, Le Corsaire, Don Quixote, Giselle, Manon, Sleeping Beauty, Swan Lake*, and many others. Ms. Kent is the recent winner of the Prix Benois de la Danse, held in Stuttgart in April 2000. Her early training included study with Hortensia Fonseca at the Academy of the Maryland Youth Ballet, and the School of American Ballet.

Benjamin Pierce joined American Ballet Theatre in 1988, leaving in 1995 for San Francisco. Since 1996 he has been a principal dancer with the San Francisco Ballet and has had leading roles in *Swan Lake, Nutcracker*, numerous Balanchine ballets, and many others. He has been a frequent guest artist for other companies and was one of the "Stars of the San Francisco Ballet" selected to perform at a gala in Bogotá, Colombia, in 1997. His training began at the age of five in Bethesda, Maryland, and continued at the Pacific Northwest Ballet School, the National Ballet of Canada, the Washington School of Ballet, where he studied with Choo San Goh, and the School of American Ballet.

Both Ms. Kent and Mr. Pierce performed for the photographs in *Physics, Dance, and the Pas de Deux* courtesy of American Ballet Theatre.

All of the photography for this book was done by Martha Swope, a name familiar to all who have contact with the dance world. Her photography has appeared in major publications from magazines to performance programs, in numerous books on dance, and in exhibits all over the world. Examples of her books are *The New York City Ballet*, with text by Lincoln Kirstein, *Baryshnikov at Work*, and *Martha Graham—Portrait of the Lady as an Artist*. Martha Swope studied ballet for five years at the School of American Ballet, and modern dance for two years with Martha Graham. She served as official photographer for the New York City Ballet for over twenty years, and for American Ballet Theatre and Martha Graham for many years. She also photographed most of the Broadway shows for years. She is now retired.

FIGURE P.4. Julie Kent and Benjamin Pierce, now principal dancers with American Ballet Theatre and San Francisco Ballet, respectively. These two dancers were the subjects for the photographs first used in *Physics, Dance, and the Pas de Deux* (1994).

All of these artists were challenged to perform their jobs in an unusual way in order to illustrate the applicable physical principles rather than purely the aesthetic imagery usually sought. They rose to these challenges with the skill, control, cooperation, and understanding that one can expect only from the most dedicated and confident artists. Martha Swope was challenged to catch on film fleeting instants of movements that one does not usually see in dance photographs. The understanding and artistic sense of all of these artists have added immeasurably to the book.

These comments would be incomplete without mention of the extraordinary privilege of working with Maribeth Anderson Payne as editor for three books over a span of almost twenty years. No author could have a more cooperative and sympathetic ear in an editor whose priorities must include both artistic quality and the business of marketability. Her judgment has always been the best combination of the idealistic and the practical.

I must once again acknowledge the great benefit I have gained from the ballet training of the Central Pennsylvania Youth Ballet (CPYB) under Marcia Dale Weary, its artistic director. She has accepted me in classes in which the next oldest dancers were sometimes fifty years younger than I! Whatever facility *and* credibility I have established in dance is due in part to the more than 5,000 ballet classes I have taken from her and the other outstanding teachers associated with the *CPYB*.

One person has had a particularly valuable effect on my recent thinking. Arleen Sugano is a gifted teacher of dance, remarkably adept at raising controversial and challenging questions and sharing profound insights, all with a disarmingly humble and whimsical manner.

Many others too numerous to mention have contributed to my evolving understanding about the physics of dance. The many wonderful people I have met in the twin worlds of physics and dance have been a source of great joy and fond memories.

Kenneth Laws

February 2001

Contents

Physics and the art of dance

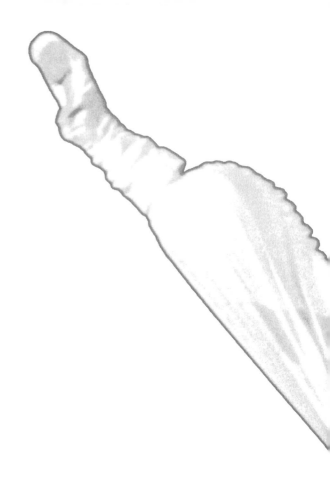

We were in the center practicing turns. (The teacher) is a natural turner, so he always says, "Don't think about it—just do it. You just turn. It's easy."

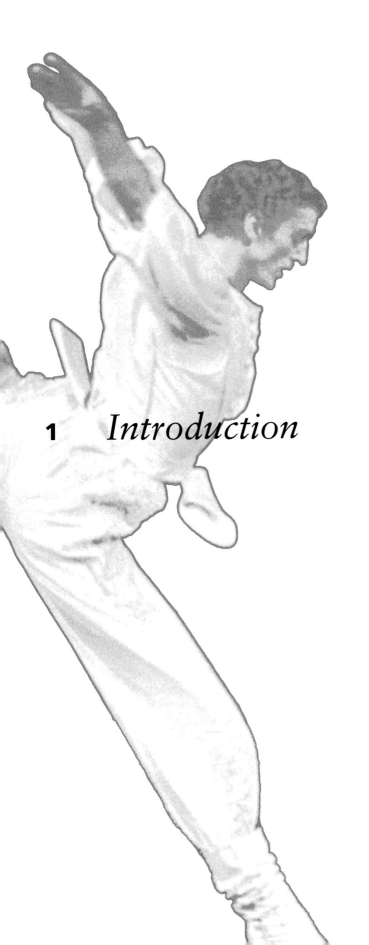

1 *Introduction*

DANCE IS AN art form intended to communicate images that appeal to the aesthetic sensibilities of observers. One might even say, "Don't think about it—just appreciate it." Dance involves creative activity, subjective and largely emotional responses to the images, and communication based on the visual language of the moving human body. Those characteristics seem to define an activity far from science, which is thought to be the realm of intellectual activity based on unemotional objectivity, involving numbers (including data derived from experiments), and analyses based on formal logic and mathematical equations. Dance is inherently visible; science often deals with phenomena invisible to the unaided human senses—X rays, DNA molecules, and supernovas in distant galaxies.

Where can one find overlap between these two realms of human activity? Can physical analysis of dance—or of any art form, for that matter—be of value to the artist or the observer, or will it only detract from the dancer's artistry or the observer's aesthetic appreciation? There is an understandable fear that the aesthetic impact of dance may be sacrificed if one tries to analyze the art form scientifically. A newspaper dance critic reporting on a scientific study of *pirouettes* headed his article "He wants to reduce ballet to a science."[1] (The investigator, who was *not* ignoring the aesthetic dimension, was appalled.)

The Role of Physical Analysis

The quote at the beginning of the chapter, reported by professional dancer Courtney Walrath, reflects a "nonthinking" approach not uncommon in ballet classes—and it sometimes works. But there are dancers who crave a deeper analysis of how to perform the movements expected of them. What *is* the role of *thinking* in dance as an art form? How do we distinguish between using scientific words to describe movement, and applying valid physical principles that give us true insights? One promising young dancer in the New York City Ballet, reflecting on the importance of his body in his profession, was quoted in the *New York Times* as saying, "My brain is

1. Daniel Webster, *Philadelphia Inquirer*, April 4, 1978, p. 4-B.

FIGURE 1.1. Sean Lavery performing for New York City Ballet in *Souvenir de Florence*. Martha Swope/TimePix.

almost worthless in my job."[2] But Bobby Boling, in his book *A Dancer's Manual*, says, "It is important to remember that nothing happens in the body without happening in the brain first. . . . Dancing is 95% mental."[3]

Many in the dance community would say that dance has to come from the heart—otherwise it's just sterile body motion. And most dancers have had the experience of analyzing some movement to death, to the point that it no longer feels like

2. Jennifer Dunning, "Daring to Own the Stage," *New York Times*, June 23, 2000.
3. Bobby Boling, *A Dancer's Manual: A Motivational Guide to Professional Dancing*, edited by Don Mirault and Keith Sellon-Wright, Tolucalake, CA: Rafter Publishing, 2000, p. 33.

dancing. How do dancers and those who observe dance balance these apparently contradictory approaches to their art and craft? How might scientific analysis be applied to dance in fruitful ways that don't compromise its aesthetic appeal?

Dancers are increasingly recognizing that they *can* benefit by understanding the framework in which human body movement must exist—a framework based on universal physical principles that apply to all moving objects. And observers can deepen, not compromise, their appreciation of the art of dance if they understand the physical basis of movement. Perhaps science and dance are not such disparate activities. According to Allegra Fuller Snyder, former head of the Dance Department at UCLA:

> Dance is more than an art. It is one of the most powerful tools for fusing the split between the two functions of the brain—the fusing of the logical with the intuitive, the fusing of the analytical perceptions with the sensorial perceptions, the fusing of holistic understanding with step by step thinking. It is a discipline which within itself deals with basic understanding of human experience, and conceptualization.[4]

First we must consider what we mean by "analysis" of dance, then describe the basic physical principles that will form the conceptual foundation. We follow with a look at the ways such analysis can benefit both dancers and others, then consider some issues of importance in the communication of scientific ideas to the dance community.

One approach to "analysis" is that of Rudolph von Laban, who created a structure in which dance movement can be codified or categorized in terms of the quality of movement (e.g., "gliding," "punching," "pressing") and the use of space (e.g., higher or lower, upstage or downstage, right or left). The aesthetic imagery determines the basis for categorization of body movements. Another type of analysis

4. Allegra Fuller Snyder, unpublished address to the faculty of the Department of Dance, University of California at Los Angeles, fall 1974.

deals with the constraints on movement imposed by the structure of the human body. The field of biomechanics involves a mechanical analysis of the movement of bodies, often dealing with the anatomy of the body and its internal workings—the way muscles and tendons apply torques to cause joints to flex or extend, for instance.

The physical analysis that constitutes the subject matter of this book deals with how the body can move within the physical constraints imposed by nature as expressed in physical laws that apply to *all* moving objects. We consider how the forces acting on the body due to gravity, the floor, or a partner determine how that body moves through space. For example, consider a dancer performing a *tour jeté*—a turning leap in which the dancer creates the image of leaping off the floor and *then* starting to turn. (See figure 1.2.) But the law of conservation of rotational momentum tells us that such a maneuver is absolutely impossible. There is, however, a subtle way the dancer can control body configuration so that the movement creates the *illusion* of a turn that occurs only after the dancer has risen into the air. Understanding the way the physical principles apply tells the dancer how to perform the movement most effectively and also provides the observer with a deeper appreciation of the dancer's skill in creating the illusion.

The Physics of Dance

What physical principles are pertinent to an analysis of dance? We must first agree that the physical laws that have been shown to apply universally to *all* moving objects do indeed apply to the moving human body, even though that body can control its own shape and the forces it exerts on its surroundings. We must therefore deal with the concepts of force, energy, momentum, inertia, velocity, and acceleration in the same careful way that these concepts have been applied to inanimate objects. The challenge is to analyze physically what *can* be analyzed in terms of appropriate physical principles, while not losing sight of the significance of the dancer's own experience—what the dancer *feels* as interactions with the world take place. The dancer ultimately controls movement by controlling his or her interaction with the

FIGURE I.2. Benjamin Pierce about to land at the end of a *tour jeté*, or *grand jeté en tournant*.

outside world. A dancer's mind determines how and when muscles are to be activated in order to produce motion (or stop it). We are considering here what happens physically after the dancer has decided to move in a particular way.

Newton's laws of motion form the basis of any analysis of moving objects. Conservation of linear and rotational momentum, and the relationship between forces and the resulting changes in the state of motion, are principles derived from Newton's laws. These concepts involve several carefully defined terms: "Force" is a term that quantifies the concept of a push or pull. "Momentum" represents a *quantity* of motion, best defined mathematically. "Linear" involves movement along a line, and "rotational" refers to a turning motion around an axis. (Note here a typical source of confusion when dancers and physicists communicate: In dance, "rotation" sometimes refers to the turnout—that is, an orientation of the leg when it is rotated outward around its longitudinal axis so that the foot points to the side. In this book "rotation" will mean the turning *motion* of any object around some rotation axis.) See appendixes A and B for quantitative descriptions of Newton's laws and associated relationships. These principles and laws are deceptively simple to state but enormously powerful when carefully applied. Such simplicity and power are sources of awesome beauty in a science such as physics.

When dancing alone, earth's gravity and the floor are the only sources of force acting on a dancer's body. All changes in the state of movement of the dancer as a whole are dependent on the forces acting on the body from gravity and from interactions between the body and the floor. The earth is pulling down on the body with a constant force; nothing one does can change that. But one *can* control the interaction with the floor so as to maintain balance or jump or start moving in some direction or start turning. Accomplishing those motions must involve an interaction between the body and the "outside world," which, in the case of a solo dancer, means gravity and the floor.

When a dancer is in contact with a partner, another source of interaction comes into play. Interaction forces between partners are controlled by two different minds, each with its own motivation, interpretation, timing, and strength. A partnered dancer now experiences forces that are no longer totally under his or her control, or even predictable, unlike interactions with the floor or gravity. This uncertainty in partnering adds to the difficulty for the dancers but can also add a sense of spontaneity very appealing to an audience.

Dance movement can be broken down into categories that involve different characteristic techniques of analysis. Some movements involve primarily vertical or horizontal motions of the body as a whole, in which rotations can be ignored. The analysis resulting from the use of simple equations of linear motion in three dimensions leads to a recognition and understanding of some interesting illusions and techniques, such as the appearance of floating horizontally in a *grand jeté*. Rotational motions require different approaches, involving the way the body's mass is distributed, different axes of rotation for different types of movement, and varied sources of forces that produce the turning motion. The simplest rotational motions are *pirouettes* of all types, but there are other movements that involve rotations around horizontal axes (*entrechats*) or skewed axes (*tour jetés*). These will be discussed in later chapters.

With careful analysis these laws can be applied to dance movement with results that are intriguing, instructive, useful, and at times surprising. Is mathematics a necessity in this analysis? Mathematical equations, although at the heart of the science of physics, are useful only when insight into the applicable physical principles is already established. Most of the material in this book deals with conceptual descriptions and illustrations of the application of physical laws. Some of the more detailed or quantitative discussions appear in the appendixes. All of these analyses are intended to be models of an approach that the reader can extend and generalize to other body movements in the infinite variety of human motion that constitutes dance.

The Value of Analysis to Dancers

Dancers are unavoidably aware of the way gravity and other interactions with their environment affect how they move. Movements must *work* physically in order for aesthetic imagery to be expressed. A graceful, ethereal, floating image will never result from a woman being lifted if the lift is inherently awkward because of where the lifting forces are applied. A climactic sudden stop at the end of a fast and energetic *pirouette* will lose its impact if there is no mechanism for quickly getting rid of the momentum of the turning motion. The mechanics of movement must work hand in hand with the aesthetic intent of the choreography.

Only when the movements called for by the choreography work within the constraints of physical reality and of the technical capabilities of the dancers can the dancers apply their interpretive skills in order to *dance*, and not just go through the motions. Then, of course, dancers strive to free their minds from concerns about the mechanics of movement, and to think about dance, movement, partner, and music rather than force, balance, inertia, and momentum.

Clearly an understanding of the mechanical principles that apply to dance movement does not automatically allow dancers to perform movements otherwise beyond their ability. The technique for achieving the balances in the Rose Adagio of the *Sleeping Beauty* may be grasped, but accomplishing those balances is still very difficult.

Dancers often push themselves to the limits of their physical capabilities. But that push is misguided if it is directed toward accomplishing something physically impossible. For instance, a tall dancer with long feet may wish to perform repetitive vertical jumps to fast music, pointing his feet while in the air and lowering his heels to the floor between jumps. As will be shown in chapter 3, that may be impossible no matter how strong the dancer is. But a short-footed dancer may have no trouble! Another dancer may be struggling to complete a half-turn in the air in a *tour jeté*. Understanding the connection between a rapid turn rate and the alignment of the body close to the rotation axis tells her how to accomplish her turn effectively. In both of these cases, understanding and working within the constraints imposed by nature and described by physical laws allows dancers to work efficiently, minimizing potential vulnerability to injury.

Achieving such an approach is not trivial. First, one has to believe in the validity of physical laws and their applicability to the human body. Bart Cook, then a member of the New York City Ballet, was quoted a number of years ago in a *Dance Magazine* interview as saying (perhaps whimsically), "It's that vision of freedom you create when you're defying physical law. . . ."[5] Second, dancers must recognize *when* it is feasible to consider physical aspects of their movements. Lisa de Ribère, a former soloist with American Ballet Theatre, who has submitted her talents to scientific scrutiny, has said that an understanding of physical principles is useful to a dancer in developing technique, but the last thing she would want to think about when on stage in front of an audience is controlling her moment of inertia or maximizing her rotational momentum in a turn! During performance, artistic sensitivities *must* occupy a dancer's full attention.

The examples used here apply to dancers working on stage or in rehearsal. But most dancers spend more time in class than on stage. How does learning take place in class? In the traditional classical ballet class, dancers learn by three means: instruction from a teacher, watching other dancers, and experimental trial and error. These traditional techniques have brought the art form to great heights, but progress can be

5. Tobi Tobias, "Bart Cook," *Dance Magazine*, September 1978, p. 59.

more efficient if *understanding* is added to the arsenal of learning tools. Knowing how physical principles apply to movement can lead dancers to figuring out logically how to solve problems. It helps to distinguish aspects of movement that are matters of style from those that directly affect the movement itself. For instance, in a *fouetté* turn sequence, the movement of the working leg from front to side once during each revolution is not only a matter of style; it has to do with the trading of momentum back and forth between different parts of the body that allows the movement to be carried out effectively.

The Value of Analysis to Observers

How can the observer of dance benefit from an understanding of applicable physical principles? First, we all have bodies, and most of us have some curiosity about how our bodies work. And we can enjoy watching other bodies move in particularly impressive ways, whether graceful or athletic or both. Consider another art form: music. We are surrounded by music in our culture. Have you ever wondered why almost all popular music is vocal? Relatively few of us play a musical instrument, but we do have voices, so we can vicariously appreciate the musical talents of those who use their voices well. Similarly, we can all appreciate the visual images created by dancers—we respond vicariously to what we can imagine ourselves doing.

Second, it is also true that an observer watching a dance performance can appreciate dance movement more deeply with an understanding of the limitations imposed by physical law and of the role of illusion. Dance movement often inspires awe in the observer, not only because of the beauty of the moving human form, but also because the dancer seems to defy normal physical constraints nature imposes on moving objects, notably ourselves. An understanding of the appropriate physical principles allows the spectator to distinguish between possible and impossible movements and to appreciate the subtle skill of a dancer who creates the illusion of performing the impossible.

Suppose one sees a *grand jeté*, as shown in figure 1.3, and marvels at the skill that allows the dancer to float horizontally for a part of this traveling leap. What is

FIGURE 1.3. Julie Kent performing a *grand jeté*, a movement so rapid that only the camera can capture and hold for our perusal the brief impressive moment at the peak of the jump.

responsible for that skill? Strength? Agility? The next deeper level of appreciation is knowing *why* that movement looks impressive: it appears to defy gravity! A body moving through the air must follow a curved trajectory, so the floating aspect must be illusory. In fact, it is the body's center of gravity (abbreviated *cg*) that must follow a curved (parabolic) trajectory. So the next level of understanding is figuring out how the dancer creates the illusion of floating. That involves understanding how he or she controls the location of the *cg* in the body so as to allow the torso and head to move horizontally while the *cg* is still following the curved trajectory. That's an identifiable skill that is understandable, though by no means easy to accomplish. But the observer's appreciation of the movement becomes deeper than "Isn't that nifty!"

A third benefit to an observer involves the source of motivation to find some appeal in what one sees on stage. We all need some "bridge" or vehicle for making that contact. For some, it is the connection with music; for others, the pure grace of human movement or portrayals of characters or culture; for some, it is the athleticism, strength, or agility; others are drawn in by knowing a participant. For some, it is seeing the way science applies to moving bodies. For those people, seeing the physical principles brought to life becomes the door to the world of dance.

Particularly appealing to people with an interest in science is to see science applied to visible, accessible, and understandable phenomena in ways that need not always be mathematical and quantitative. For instance, raising the arms during push-off for a vertical jump (shown in figure 1.4) produces a higher jump because of the vertical momentum stored in the arms while the feet are still pushing off from the floor. The sudden comprehension of that kind of process and explanation can be quite thrilling and involves physical insight rather than equations or quantitative data. Such insight allows the observer to see the subtleties in the apparently simple process of dancers jumping vertically.

Analysis for Teachers and Health Professionals

The value of one aspect of analysis has gained full acceptance during the last dozen years. Dancers, dance teachers, and people in the health professions are now recognizing the importance of a knowledge of anatomy for allowing dancers to use their bodies most effectively and safely. Dance medicine specialists, rather than just treating injuries, are increasingly recommending to dancers strategies for staying healthy. For all in the dance world, a knowledge of anatomical limitations and constraints on human body movement can help prevent the kinds of injuries that interrupt or end many promising dance careers.

Teachers benefit from understanding how the muscles work in dance movement; what constraints are imposed by muscles, bones, and joints; and to what extent a young dance student can expand the range of motion permitted by these constraints. An example is a *grand battement devant* in which the structure of the hip prevents maintaining a complete turnout through the upper range of the motion. The sensible teacher knows and teaches the ideal positions and body configurations but recognizes the distinction between the ideal and the possible. Teaching involves a balance between aspiring to elicit the best technique from dancers and recognizing human limits.

FIGURE 1.4. Benjamin Pierce and Abi Stafford, two dancers of noticeably different sizes, performing a vertical jump. Some questions arise: Why do they raise their arms for the jump? Why is Benjamin jumping higher than Abi? Does he take longer to complete his jump?

Physical analyses can make important contributions to an understanding of the effects of the size of dancers on the movements they can perform—the vertical jumps, for instance, shown in figure 1.4. Most choreographers and teachers recognize that small dancers do have different ways of moving than taller ones, but just what are the differences? How can teachers avoid expecting the impossible of tall dancers, or choreographers maximize the effectiveness of their use of performers of different sizes? Are there physical principles that make the slender, long-legged "Balanchine" dancers particularly appropriate for Balanchine choreography? Is there a way to choreograph specifically for the talented but "undersized" dancers who can outperform their taller counterparts in certain movements and tempos?

Communication: Words, Images, and Photographs

One of the challenges in dealing with technical aspects of dance involves the uses of appropriate vocabulary and terminology. How is a basis for communication established between such disparate fields as physics and dance? One characteristic of science is that it is built on precise definitions of pertinent terms. These definitions are intended to be as objective as possible so that they are universally usable, independent of the unique interpretations of individuals. Physicists may disagree on interpretations of observations, but they depend on an assumed agreement concerning the definitions of the terms.

People dealing with dance depend on language to serve two functions. One is to be a vehicle for communicating ideas from one person to another. The second is to form meaningful images in terms of dancers' individual senses of body and movement. A dance teacher may use words that have objective definitions, but unless students can translate those words into images applicable to their own bodies, the information transfer is abstract and not useful.

Individual students, because of different ages and backgrounds, have different levels and kinds of understanding. Dance teachers, who often deal with young people who have not developed a sophisticated vocabulary, create images that seem to work, building on common understandings of how it "feels" to perform certain movements or maintain certain body positions. "Feel as if your body is squeezed into a drinking straw" may be translated by some students into "Maintain a compact alignment around a vertical axis in order to perform a controlled turn." Or, more physical yet, "Minimize your rotational inertia around a vertical axis so that the torque and rotational momentum needed for a given rate of turn will be minimized." The message is the same; the frame of reference is determined by the student's background and intellectual capacity. (The physical principles applicable to the *pirouette* are discussed in chapter 4 and appendixes A and B.)

Another comment often heard in pirouette instruction is to stretch vertically, pushing into the floor with the supporting foot while reaching for the ceiling with the head. Now if the vertical height of the center of gravity is constant, then the vertical force of the dancer's foot against the floor is no greater and no less than the body weight. But the image produced by that instruction elicits a response in the dancer to "pull up," producing a strong and straight vertical alignment, again decreasing the rotational inertia for a substantial rate of turn. Mass displaced from the rotation axis contributes to a wobbling, since that mass tends to be thrown out from the axis by a centrifugal effect. Good body placement is thus not only desirable for aesthetic reasons, but is also necessary to achieve a reasonable turn rate and smooth, stable rotation.

How are the concepts of movement analysis dealt with in a medium as static as a book? Good dance photography involves a subtle challenge to portray movement with static visual displays. The challenge is particularly crucial when the purpose of the photography is to illustrate the applicability of physical principles, which apply mostly to moving bodies. The transitions and accelerations from one configuration to the next are particularly amenable to the type of physical analysis that is especially fruitful in contributing to an understanding of dance movement. But how does one illustrate these transitions visually? An example is a *degagé/tombé* movement (discussed in chapter 3 and illustrated in figure 3.4), which contributes to a horizontal acceleration away from a balance condition. A still photograph of the movement in progress shows the lean of the body that is related to the acceleration; the viewer has to imagine the motion associated with the position in order to grasp the full significance of the illustration. Martha Swope's photographs in this book are the most effective way of presenting such visual images.

Certainly we do not expect to "reduce ballet to a science." The world of dance is large and complex, with many windows through which one can both perceive and illuminate. Through these windows one may see portrayals of characters or images of a culture, spectacular athleticism or lyrical grace, painful years of dancers' discipline or free expression of human creativity. I hope that the view through the window of physical analysis will enhance, not detract from, the depth of appreciation this art form can inspire, as well as contribute to the advancement of the art and skill of dance.

2   BALANCE

You are a dancer about to end your solo on a very shallow stage. As you end with a flourish, you discover to your horror that your feet are an inch from the edge of the stage! In fact you are off balance, about to topple into the orchestra pit, where the percussionist is already scrambling out of the way. Just as you are wondering if you'll bounce off the kettledrum or crash through it, your reflexes take over and try to keep you from falling.

What do you think will happen? Are you doomed to take a tumble into the timpani?

WHAT ROLE DOES balance play in dance, other than preventing a tumble off the edge of a stage? Any choreographed dance consists of three components: movement, poses, and transitions. Movement is the heart of dance and the primary aspect that portrays the style and image that a dance conveys. But some of the more dramatic moments occur when a dancer enters a balanced pose and holds the position *en pointe* for several heart-stopping seconds. A *pirouette* ending in a motionless balanced pose is particularly impressive. Analyzing the techniques a person must use in order to achieve or maintain balance, or to regain lost balance, involves some intriguing physics and demonstrates that some unexpected and counterintuitive actions are needed.

First, what does it mean to be "balanced"? For our purposes, balance means that the body is in stationary equilibrium with no tendency to topple due to the effect of gravity. We will see that a body is balanced if its center of gravity is directly above the area of support at the floor. "Center of gravity"? "Area of support"? We will explore these concepts in the next section.

Condition for Static Balance

We will define "center of gravity" as "that point where the downward force of gravity appears to act on the body as a whole." It is related to what a dancer calls his or her "center," which is a more subjectively defined concept but is also related to balance.

What determines the location of the center of gravity? For a person in a normal standing position on two feet, the center of gravity is in the sagittal plane (the vertical plane that divides the left and right sides of the body), somewhere in the abdominal area. It is somewhat higher in the body in men than in women, due to greater hip mass in women and chest/shoulder mass in men. Now suppose part of the body, such as a leg, is extended to the side. That displacement of part of the mass of the body to the side and up will cause the center of gravity also to be displaced to that side and up. To remain balanced, at least part of the mass of the rest of the body must be displaced in the opposite horizontal direction, which may cause the bal-

FIGURE 2.1.
Sandra Jennings in a New York
City Ballet performance of
Bournonville Divertissements.
Martha Swope/TimePix.

anced body to lean away from the extended leg. In any balanced position, different dancers find that slightly different positions of the body work best, due to differences in body structure, flexibility, and comfort.

Now what do we mean by "area of support at the floor"? If one is standing on one foot, the meaning is obvious, and the body will be balanced if its center of gravity lies on a vertical line that passes through that contact area of the foot on the floor. Now suppose one is standing on two feet on the floor, both pointing forward and separated by some lateral distance. The area of support is the area lying within a boundary formed by the outside edges of the two feet, a line joining the two sets of toes, and a line joining the two heels. A person is balanced if the center of gravity lies directly above a point anywhere within that defined area.

Clearly if the area of support is small, as when the feet are close together, or *very* small, as for a dancer on one foot *en pointe*, it is a great challenge to locate the center of gravity within the range of locations directly above that small area, and toppling off balance is hard to avoid. At the opposite extreme, a three-point stance of an offensive lineman in football (on two feet and one hand) is a very stable configuration.

Stability and balance, or lack thereof, are related to turnout, that characteristic position of the legs and feet that is so important in classical ballet. Suppose a dancer is in first position, with the feet heel to heel pointing sideways directly away from each other. It is not much of a challenge to keep the lateral position of the center of gravity somewhere between the outer ends of the feet. So sideways stability is easy to achieve. But stability for backward or forward displacements is far more precarious, as one has no more than the width of the feet for the range of position of the center of gravity that will produce equilibrium. Fifth position (one foot in front of and touching the other, heel to toe and toe to heel) is not as stable as first position for side-to-side displacement but is more stable for fore-and-aft movement of the center of gravity. Fourth position (like fifth but with the feet separated front-to-back) is more stable than fifth, which perhaps explains its common use as preparation for *pirouettes*.

One important characteristic of the center of gravity is that it cannot be moved from rest unless some net force acts on the body as a whole. That is, one can move individual parts of the body relative to each other in many ways, but unless those movements result in a force between the body and the "outside world" (everything outside the body itself), then those movements can result in no change in the location of the center of gravity in space. If one is standing still on a floor, there *are* forces acting on the body—the downward force of gravity acting at the center of gravity, and the upward force of the floor supporting the person. But these two forces acting on the body balance each other, acting along the same vertical line, producing no net movement of the center of gravity. And if one is standing on ice with infinitely slippery shoes, there is no horizontal force either, so no movement of the center of gravity of the body can occur.

More accurately, unless the outside world exerts a force on a body, there is no *change in state of motion of the body*. That is, if the body's center of gravity is at rest, it will remain at rest. But if it is initially moving, it will remain in uniform motion until it is acted on by some outside force. For example, an ice skater moving in a straight line on almost frictionless ice will continue moving with constant speed as long as no forces act on the body. This powerful result is described by the first of Newton's three laws, mentioned in the previous chapter and discussed more fully in appendix A.

Suppose a dancer starts on one foot *en pointe*, in an *arabesque* position as shown in figure 2.2. And suppose she is initially balanced, as shown on the left side of figure 2.3, so that her center of gravity is on a vertical line that passes through the area of contact between her *pointe* shoe and the floor. If she is absolutely motionless, she could presumably remain there forever. But there *is* motion—breathing, beating heart, and circulating blood if nothing else. So it is likely that she will soon find herself slightly off balance, beginning to topple, as in the right view in figure 2.3.

If the center of gravity is close to that "balance area," the acceleration away from the vertical is initially quite small. In other words, the closer a dancer is to a perfect balance, the slower will be the fall away from balance. If there is a small initial angle by which the line from the support to the center of gravity is displaced from the vertical, that angle will increase at an accelerating rate. The calculations in appendix E are applied to the geometry of typical dancers. The results show that the angle of departure from the vertical increases by a factor of about eight in 1 second after the initial "almost balanced" moment. If the initial angle is 1°, the angle after 1 second will be about 8°, whereas if the initial angle is 4°, the body 1 second later makes an angle of more than 30° from the vertical, which probably implies a crisis requiring some immediate corrective action. Since these two examples represent a difference in initial position of the center of gravity of perhaps 2 inches, the initial placement of the body must be quite accurate if temporary balance is to be achieved.

Now suppose a dancer is standing on one foot with the heel down and wishes to rise onto *pointe*. How does she remain balanced? Since the supporting foot does

FIGURE 2.2.
Julie Kent balanced in an *arabesque* position. Toppling will begin if her center of gravity is not directly above the small area of contact between her *pointe* shoe and the floor.

not move, the area of support at the floor must follow the contact area. If the center of gravity is initially over the back of the foot near the heel, then that location must be shifted nearly the length of the foot if balance is to be maintained when on *pointe*. If, however, the weight is forward toward the toe before the dancer rises onto *pointe*, then that shift in position of the center of gravity is smaller and more easily managed.

Regaining Balance

Let us assume that the dancer wishes to remain balanced. What, if anything, can she do to regain balance if she starts to topple? There are only two mechanisms for such adjustment. The area of support at the floor must be relocated so that it falls di-

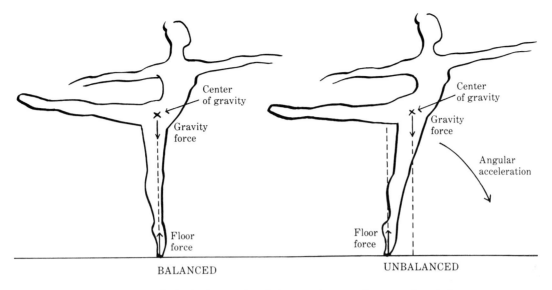

FIGURE 2.3. Forces acting on the body that result in balance or in a toppling away from balance.

rectly under the center of gravity, or the center of gravity must be shifted so that it is over the area of support at the floor.

The location of the contact area between the foot and the floor can be controlled. Of course the dancer may hop, shifting the horizontal position of the entire supporting foot, or step down onto the second foot. But a more subtle adjustment is possible. The center of force may be defined as that point where a distributed force or a collection of several forces may be considered to act, in terms of its effect on a body. When one balances on a flat foot, one can feel the foot moving in such a way as to make small corrections in the location of that center of force within the area of support, thereby maintaining the center of support under the center of gravity, as shown in figure 2.4. A dancer *en pointe*, however, has such a small area of contact with the floor that it is quite difficult to shift the center of force. The difficulty of the required manipulation is one reason dancing *en pointe* requires strong feet and ankles and much skill!

The other technique for regaining balance involves shifting the location of the center of gravity back toward the vertical line above the contact area at the floor. We have noted that controlling the location of the center of gravity requires some

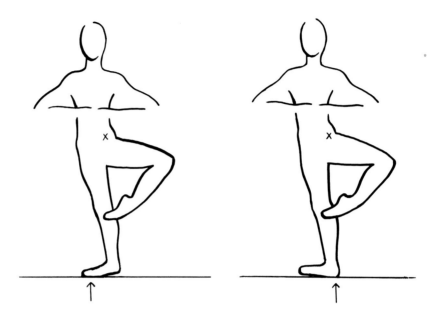

FIGURE 2.4. Shifting the center of supporting force at the floor in order to control balance.

force from the "outside world" acting on the body, so no manipulation of the body will accomplish the desired end unless it produces such a force. A remarkable implication of that fact is that it does no good merely to try to move a massive part of the body in the desired direction directly. That may only result in some other part of the body being displaced in the opposite direction.

Recall now the predicament described at the beginning of this chapter. Let's try an experiment simulating that situation of starting to fall from the edge of the stage. Allow yourself to start toppling forward from a standing position, and see how your body instinctively reacts to keep you from falling (without simply stepping forward). With a keen but incomplete sense of mechanical analysis you may move the upper body backward, recognizing that a movement of body mass backward must be accomplished in order to move the center of gravity back toward the balance location. Over you go into the kettledrum!

If you succeeded in correcting the imbalance, you probably relaxed and found that an automatic reaction of the body took over. You bent the upper body suddenly *forward* from the waist, and perhaps also rotated the arms in a windmill fashion (forward and down, back and up). Why did those movements succeed? The body tries to conserve its rotational momentum around a horizontal axis through the center of gravity in the abdominal area. (See appendix B for a discussion of the conservation of rotational momentum.) That rotational momentum is approximately zero when toppling first begins. Now if the upper body rotates forward from the hips, and perhaps the arms rotate in the same direction (counterclockwise as viewed from your left, as in figure 2.5), the rest of the body will try to rotate in the opposite direction (clockwise as viewed from the left) in order to retain the zero total rotational momentum. Thus, the legs will try to rotate forward from the hips, pushing forward with the feet against the floor. By Newton's third law, that results in the floor exerting a force backward against your feet. If that's the only horizontal force acting on you, it will act in such a way as to move your center of gravity backward, returning it toward the balance condition! Thus, the reactions of the body—moving the upper body in the direction of the fall, and perhaps also rotating the arms—are surprisingly the movements that work, and the mechanism can be understood on the basis of known physical principles. And you have succeeded in preventing yourself from falling off the stage into the timpani!

Although dancers may intuitively realize that it *is* possible to regain balance while supported on one foot, they may fail to recognize that it is not the manipulations of the body directly that restore balance but the resulting horizontal force exerted on the floor that accomplishes the shift in position of the center of gravity. That is, movements of the body that maximize the horizontal force of the supporting foot against the floor will be most effective in restoring balance. Unless such movements occur, the body may move in counterproductive ways, preventing the desired adjustment in balance. In fact, the natural and correct reaction for regaining balance, as described above, has been claimed to be wrong, and dancers have been admonished to overcome that "instinct" and merely move the body back toward balance, clearly a counterproductive action.[1] Fortunately, most people, including

1. Norman Thomson, "The Barre—Aid or Crutch?" *Dance Magazine*, March 1981.

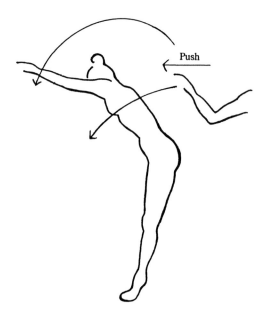

FIGURE 2.5. The body's reaction to being pushed off balance toward the front. The upper-body rotation shown here works in allowing the body to regain balance.

dancers, have developed a valid automatic reaction, probably learned in early childhood, for regaining or maintaining balance.

Dancers can be observed to carry out those necessary adjustments when trying to balance alone. Of course the movements are subtle because dancers, among all categories of people who depend on control of body movement for their activity, are perhaps *most* sensitive to the condition of balance or loss thereof.

What can dancers learn from this analysis? First, the upper body must be kept strong but loose enough that those subtle movements can indeed be carried out. Locking the body rigidly in position in the hope that balance will be maintained is counterproductive. Second, smaller manipulations of the upper body are necessary if the rotational inertia is increased by holding parts of the body farther from its center of gravity. Extended arms make regaining balance easier for the same reason that tightrope walkers carry a long pole. That is, the pole has a large rotational inertia around a horizontal axis, so that twisting it one way or the other will produce a significant sideways force against the tightrope without the pole responding with a large rotation.

Third, the higher the center of gravity is above the floor, the slower the toppling rate. Therefore, holding the arms high and the gesture leg at the knee of the supporting leg makes regaining balance easier by allowing the necessary adjustments to be carried out before the departure from balance has become very great. But other factors, like the relative discomfort of one position compared to another, may mask that effect.

There are other, more familiar applications of this analysis of the mechanism for regaining balance. If you have ever walked along a rail of a railroad track, you have probably found that if you start falling to your right, your upper body will suddenly bend toward the right. That movement results in the rail's exerting a horizontal force on your body toward the left, helping you to return to balance.

Balance while Rotating

An interesting situation arises when a dancer performs a *pirouette* while maintaining balance. Is it possible—or even necessary—for an unbalanced, *rotating* dancer to make the subtle corrections described above for returning to a balanced condition?

If the body rotates fast enough, like a spinning top, loss of balance will result in a wobbling action ("precession" of the rotation axis around the vertical) rather than toppling. The analysis described in appendix F shows that the rotation rate is *not* sufficiently rapid in a normal *pirouette*, and toppling will indeed occur unless adjustments are made similar to those that worked when the body was not rotating.

The challenge for the rotating, unbalanced dancer is to try to adjust the body position in a way that corrects the imbalance as if the body were not rotating. The task is made more difficult by the rotation because the adjustment, which must have a particular direction in space, must change relative to the body as the body turns. For instance, suppose, as shown in figure 2.6, that the body is off balance leaning toward stage right while turning to the right. The body must adjust its position in such a way that the floor will exert a horizontal force on the body toward stage left in order to shift the center of gravity back to the vertical line over the area of support. So, as shown in figure 2.6, Lisa de Ribère must rotate her upper body toward stage right. But that direction quickly changes from *her* right to *her* front, to *her* left, and so on.

Is it possible for a dancer to make these adjustments while turning at perhaps two or three revolutions per second? Perhaps so, because the initial movement of the body is what results in the force that can produce a return to balance, and, if it works, the body can return to the upright position. But if such an adjustment is *not* possible that quickly, then the dancer must begin the turn sufficiently close to balance that such adjustments are unnecessary. That also is a lot to expect of a dancer! A relaxed upper body is necessary to allow for the subtle body adjustments, but a strong lower body provides the support that prevents unwanted "wavering."

So how is it possible for some dancers to accomplish a multiple *pirouette* of a dozen or so turns without falling? The answer probably involves a combination of several factors. First, the dancer does have to be close enough to balance that at least the first few turns can be accomplished with no adjustment. These turns may indeed be rapid enough that there is some stabilizing effect as with a spinning top that remains upright because it is spinning. (Such a rapid turn with a rigid body is performed by an ice skater doing very rapid spins.) But as the turns become slower because of friction, one can look for those shifts of body position that do change direction relative to the body as the body turns. This can be observed in a dancer skilled at *pirouettes*, who is asked to try to maintain a turn even when falling out of it. Such a dancer, when performing pirouettes significantly off balance, can be observed to carry out the strange-looking body adjustments that do indeed rotate relative to the body in order to maintain a constant direction in space. Such adjusting motions must occur so rapidly that they may be impossible to teach, meaning that certain people who are "natural" turners have, or can feel and develop, the proper reactions, and others must depend on initial accurate balance in order to accomplish the more common two- or three-turn *pirouettes*.

A Final Look

The fundamental techniques used here for analyzing situations involving balance can be applied to an infinite variety of positions. The sources of forces and torques that maintain balance must be identified, then the action of the body that will cause the required forces to be exerted must be found. For the situations described in this chapter, there are a number of ways dancers and dance teachers can think about solutions to the problems. First, in achieving a condition of balance, the center of gravity of the body must be on a vertical line that passes within the area of support at the floor. In an *arabesque penché*, for instance, in which the mass of the body shifts forward as the leg rises toward the vertical and the torso leans forward, the dancer must allow the hip area to shift to the rear so that the body's center of gravity remains over the supporting foot. The situation is somewhat different with the support of a partner, as will be discussed in chapter 6.

When the condition of balance is not quite met, the body can carry out adjusting motions so as to regain balance. These adjustments require either a shift in location of the center of vertical supporting force at the floor or a push horizontally against the floor in a direction such as to cause the body's center of gravity to return to the balance configuration. The former is accomplished by adjustments in the supporting ankle or foot; the latter, by rotating the upper body *toward* the direction of fall. Relaxation of the upper body can contribute to a sensitivity to slight departures from balance and make the adjustments appear more subtle to the observer.

Balancing while rotating is made difficult by the fact that the direction of adjustment necessary to regain lost balance must shift relative to the body's orientation if it is to have the desired direction relative to the world. That is, if the body is tending to fall toward stage right, the direction of adjustments in body position must remain such as to restore the body toward stage left even while it is rotating relative to the stage.

What goes on in the mind of a dancer trying to maintain a balanced pose for a dramatically long time? Is the dancer thinking, "Gee, I seem to be falling to my

right, so I know I must quickly move my upper body to the right in order to exert a force toward the right between my feet and the floor so that the floor exerts a force to the left on my body, returning me to the balance condition in which my center of gravity is on a vertical line passing through my support at the floor"? Probably not! But somewhere in the mind of the dancer there is an automatic response that accomplishes exactly that! It is remarkable that the mind/body system is capable of that sort of rapid and automatic response, particularly in the case of dancers, who are known to be particularly sensitive to balance and particularly adept at maintaining balance.

FIGURE 2.6. Sequential views showing the dancer's reaction to an off-balance *pirouette*. The direction of the correction must remain constant in space and therefore must rotate relative to the body as the body rotates. These four posed views, although exaggerated, show the directions of body adjustments that must be made to correct balance in a *pirouette* off balance to the left of the picture. Viewed from left to right, these photos represent an *en dehors pirouette* turning to the right.

The series of *arabesque penchés* on a sloping ramp in *La Bayadere*, a long held *arabesque* pose *en pointe* in the Sugar Plum Fairy *pas de deux* from the *Nutcracker*, and Giselle's shifting *attitude* position while hopping *en pointe* along a diagonal— all have similar requirements for maintaining balance that can be understood using these principles. The same principles apply to the infinite variety of balanced poses seen in other styles of dance.

3   MOTIONS

without turns

In your next solo you find yourself dreading the approaching series of vertical jumps, beating your legs together while in the air. The conductor can't seem to get the tempo right! In rehearsal you asked him for a faster tempo, and you couldn't keep up with the music. But when you asked him to slow it down, you couldn't seem to jump high enough to keep from getting ahead of the music.

You recall the exasperated conductor saying, "But my electronic timer says I slowed the tempo by only 10 percent—that's hardly noticeable! You mean you can't just jump 10 percent higher and stay with the music?"

Was the conductor's assessment of the situation accurate?

UCH OF DANCE involves dancers traveling through space, both horizontally and vertically. A number of questions arise when we analyze such movements, first without the complicating presence of rotations. How does a dancer initiate horizontal movement from rest? As we saw in the last chapter, the dancer's center of gravity remains at rest unless there is a force *from outside the body* acting *on* the body. And if there is no partner, the floor is the only source of such a force. We will see that there is more than one way of making the floor push horizontally on the dancer in order to initiate movement. Once the body is moving, we may want to change its direction and eventually stop it, again requiring forces from the floor.

Simple vertical jumps are not so simple! We will find the relationship between the height of a jump and the time in the air, see the effect of the use of the arms in increasing the height of a jump, and analyze the vertical forces necessary for jumping to a particular height and the forces acting on the body upon landing.

Interesting things happen when we combine horizontal and vertical motions. Indeed, a dancer *can* create the illusion of floating horizontally through the air, defying gravity! Techniques for performing the most effective *grandes jetés* arise from this analysis. Finally, we will consider the important characteristics of dance floors.

Acceleration from Rest

First, let us consider how a dancer can begin a horizontal movement from rest, involving a quick acceleration away from a standing position. As we found in the discussion of balance (chapter 2), if the body's center of gravity lies on a vertical line above the area of support, and there are no horizontal forces acting on the body, it will be in equilibrium and will remain at rest. If there *is* a net horizontal force, an acceleration of the body will occur that is proportional to the force and in the same direction.

Now how does a person arrange to have a force exerted on himself in order to accelerate? For every force exerted by a body against something, the body experiences an equal and opposite force acting back on itself (Newton's third law, de-

FIGURE 3.1. Takako Asakawa, of the Martha Graham Company, in *Diversion of Angels*. Martha Swope/TimePix.

scribed in more detail in appendix A). Since the floor is the only source of force accessible to the solo dancer, he must arrange to push against the floor in order to accelerate. How does he do that? One mechanism is to *shift the center of force between the feet and the floor*. Recall that the center of force is defined as the point where a distributed force, or a collection of several forces, may be considered to act. That is, if one's weight is distributed evenly over the supporting foot while it is flat on the floor, the center of force would be in the center of the foot. Leaning forward so that the weight is on the ball of the foot shifts the center of force toward the front of the foot. If the weight is distributed evenly between *two* feet, one in front of the other, the center of force would be halfway between the feet; if more of the weight is borne by the front foot, the center of force would shift toward the front foot.

Now suppose one wishes to accelerate forward from a standing position. If the feet are spread apart to the front and back, as in a lunge or a wide fourth position, merely lifting the front foot will shift the effective center of force to the rear. (See the diagrams in figure 3.2.) The center of gravity is then well in front of the support, and a fall to the front begins. The back foot can then exert a backward push against the floor, which converts the toppling into a horizontal acceleration.

If the feet are together at the beginning of the movement, the acceleration takes longer, since the center of force cannot be shifted as far horizontally. If the center of gravity is initially over the balls of the feet when the dancer is balanced, and then he lifts the front of the feet, the center of gravity will be slightly in front of the new center of force. A toppling rotation will start, as shown in figure 3.3, which can be counteracted if the feet push backward against the floor and the floor consequently pushes forward against the feet. That force begins the linear acceleration forward and also produces a torque that counteracts the rotation induced by the force of gravity acting in front of the supporting feet. But because the center of gravity is only slightly in front of the center of force, the toppling rate will be small, and the horizontal force that can be exerted by the feet against the floor is small. If that force is too large, the feet will simply run out from under the body, destroying equilibrium. The horizontal force must be just great enough to counteract the toppling.

A familiar example of this mechanism for acceleration is the starting position for a sprinter. Much of the runner's weight is forward on the hands, so that when the hands are lifted, the center of gravity is far forward of the supporting feet, and a large horizontal accelerating force can be exerted by the feet without the feet running out from under the rest of the body. Note, however, that a racing dive in swimming does not allow for as rapid an acceleration, because the distance through which the center of force can be shifted is limited by the small size of the diving platform.

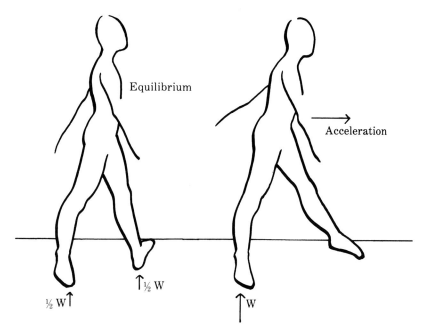

FIGURE 3.2. Shifting location of supporting force from two feet to one foot, producing a horizontal acceleration.

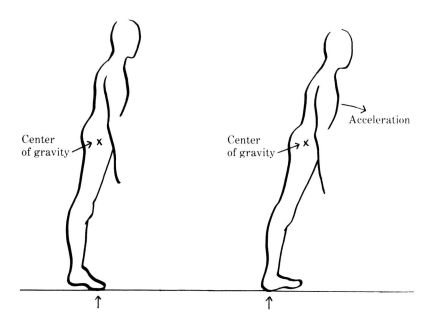

FIGURE 3.3. Shifting center of supporting force, destroying balance and allowing for a horizontal acceleration.

A related mechanism is almost obvious. The center of force can be shifted to a location behind the center of gravity by moving the back foot farther back, then pushing off with it.

The second mechanism for accelerating from rest involves *thrusting one leg front*, as in a *degagé* movement often seen at the beginning of a moving combination, and illustrated by Sean Lavery in figure 3.4. Recall that an off-balance person can regain balance by rotating a part of the body in one direction, which causes another part of the body to try to rotate in the opposite direction, pushing against the floor and causing the floor to push against the body in the direction needed to restore the center of gravity to the balance position above the area of support. In this case, the dancer *wants* to destroy balance in order to start toppling, which allows for the acceleration. That *degagé* represents a rotation of one leg forward around a horizontal axis through the hip, which causes the other leg to try to rotate backward to balance the rotational momentum. That backward push of the supporting foot against the floor results in a forward force from the floor on the body, producing the forward acceleration of the body. This mechanism can exist only for the short time that one part of the body (the *degagé* leg in this case) is *accelerating* relative to the rest of the body. But once the center of gravity is displaced, the body will continue to topple.

A motionless dancer, then, in order to accelerate rapidly with the first beat of the music, must quickly exert a backward force against the floor. The weight should be forward on the toes, or, better yet, one foot should be well in front of the other. Lifting the front foot will allow for a fast acceleration forward from the initial position. The movement will be more effective if the dancer also swings the front leg toward the front as the acceleration begins. And of course all of these general principles can be applied to sideways or backward accelerations.

Motion in a Curved Path

Technically, the term "acceleration" refers to any change in velocity, whether an increase or a decrease in speed *or* a change in the *direction* of motion. These accelerations require forces acting on the dancer from outside the body. One such horizon-

FIGURE 3.4. Sean Lavery performing a *tombé*, or lunge, which produces a horizontal force between the push-off foot and the floor, resulting in a horizontal acceleration.

tal acceleration involves motion in a circular path, around the stage, for instance. Auto racing tracks are banked at the curves in order to allow the appropriate horizontal accelerating force to be exerted without the car skidding.

As we have seen, in order for a dancer to achieve a horizontal acceleration, the center of gravity must be displaced from the vertical line over the center of support at the floor, so that the floor can exert a horizontal force. As a dancer travels around the stage in a circular path, there must be a force on the body from the floor directed toward the center of the circle. That force will cause the constant change in direction of motion that is needed for the curved path. Because of the significant velocity, and because the circle diameter is restricted by the stage size, a sizable lean toward the center is often needed to prevent moving off the circle "on a tangent," perhaps leaving the stage precipitously. Note Sean's lean in figure 3.5, as he moves in the curved path described. The angle of lean can be calculated and is in fact independent of the dancer's height, weight, or shape. If he is traveling at about 15 feet per second (half the speed of a sprinter) in a circle of diameter 30 feet, he must lean toward the center at an angle of 25 degrees from the vertical! The horizontal force between his feet and the floor must be almost half his weight. The frictional properties of floors that allow that magnitude of horizontal force will be discussed shortly.

Note that no change in horizontal speed *or direction* is possible during the flight phase of a traveling jump, when there is no contact with the floor. Horizontal travel in a curved path before a jump will not result in a curved path during the flight, much to the dismay of one trying to leap near the back of a stage without obliterating scenery, props, or corps members! The apparently curved motion described above actually consists of a series of flights following trajectories above straight lines on the floor, with brief moments of contact with the floor during which the direction of motion is changed.

Stopping Horizontal Motion

A dancer moving across the floor may wish to stop moving, disposing of all of the linear momentum. Again, the floor is the source of the decelerating (slowing) force when the body leans back so that the center of gravity is to the rear of the support, allowing the floor to exert a retarding force to slow the forward motion. One often sees a traveling combination ending with a jump to one landing foot. The landing on the extended front foot allows for a forward force against the floor, which results in the appropriate retarding force of the floor against the body. That retarding force allows the forward velocity to decrease to zero, hopefully just as the body reaches a balanced equilibrium.

FIGURE 3.5. Moving in a curved path requires a force from the floor toward the center of curvature. The lean of Sean Lavery's body shown here allows for that force when his feet are on the ground between leaps. The situation is similar to the banking of a curved road that allows cars to follow the turn without skidding.

Vertical Jumps

Vertical jumps are movements common to all forms of dance and, in fact, any athletic activity. In these jumps the body spends some time in the air with no contact with the floor or ground, returning to the surface close to the departure point. Unlike a simple object such as a ball, the human body can change its configuration during the time in the air, giving rise to some interesting phenomena.

Most long-footed dancers have experienced difficulty when asked to perform rapid vertical jumps. These jumps must be performed in the rhythm of the music, with reasonable elevation and, particularly in ballet, pointed feet in the air and heels on the floor between jumps. Sometimes these requirements are physically incompatible, and compromises must be made!

All jumps involve vertical accelerations and forces. Because gravity acts vertically downward on our bodies at all times, we can remain motionless only if there is a vertical supporting force equal to our weight. In order to jump off the ground vertically we need to exert a force downward against the floor *greater* than our weight, for long enough to achieve the vertical upward velocity desired. Although small vertical velocities may be achieved with the feet alone, most jumps require an acceleration from bent legs—a *plié* position.

The height of a jump depends on the downward vertical force exerted against the floor and on the length of time or vertical distance through which that force is exerted. That is, when the body is at the lowest *plié* before the jump, the center of gravity is at a height h_1. When the feet leave the floor in the jump, the force against the floor ceases, and the center of gravity is at a height we identify as h_2. When the dancer has reached the maximum height and is about to descend back to the floor, his center of gravity is at a height h_3. The vertical distance through which the force is exerted is $h_2 - h_1$, which we will call d. We will define the height H of the jump as $h_3 - h_2$. Now let R be the ratio, assumed constant during push-off, between the vertical force exerted against the floor and the dancer's weight. (If the two are equal, $R = 1$ and there's no jump; if the dancer exerts a vertical force of twice his weight, $R = 2$.) The height of the jump is then given by

$$H = d(R - 1).$$

If a *plié* lowers the center of gravity 1 foot, then a vertical force of double one's weight will allow for a jump in which the center of gravity rises 1 foot above the value when the dancer leaves the floor. Of course, the assumption that the force is constant during the upward acceleration is a crude one, but if we mean the *average* force exerted during that time, the general results are valid and illuminating. Studies have shown, however, that *too* deep a *plié* decreases the average force that can be exerted, and there is actually some sacrifice in the height of the resulting jump. Of course, what is "too deep" depends on an individual dancer's strength. And the movement leading to the jump is important also, since a jump from a *plié* at rest is less effective than a jump moving into and out of the *plié* in one smooth motion in which the vertical force against the floor is already established before the ascent starts.

Recall that the height of a jump can be related to the magnitude of the net vertical force acting on the body and the length of time the force acts. Suppose that concept is applied to the use of the arms during the takeoff phase of a jump. In fact, some dancers start with the arms extended out to the side, then bring them down and then up overhead as the *plié* and subsequent push-off occur. Dancers who do that either extend the length of time the force of the floor is exerted on the body or make the force greater. The reason is that the arms are storing more vertical momentum while they are rising relative to the rest of the body than they would if they did not have that relative motion. When the arms reach their full extended height, then that stored momentum is transferred back to the body as a whole, producing more total vertical momentum of the body, resulting in a higher jump. Studies have shown[1] that larger, stronger dancers tend to increase the vertical force between the feet and the floor, while smaller dancers tend to increase the length of time they are pushing against the floor. Perhaps that is because smaller dancers push with a force closer to the maximum possible than larger dancers. Is use of the arms effective? The same study shows that the net gain, although quite variable, averaged about 25 percent in a group of ten dancers of various sizes and ages and both genders.

An important consideration in jumps involves the timing, determined by the rhythm of the music. Here the length of time the body is in the air depends *only* on the height of the jump, not on the body size or weight, since the acceleration due to gravity is the same for all weights. (See appendix A for a mathematical analysis

1. Kenneth Laws and Caren Petrie, "Momentum Transfer in Dance Movement—Vertical Jumps: A Research Update," *Medical Problems of Performing Artists* 14, no. 3 (September 1999): 138–40.

of vertical jumps.) But the relationship is not linear. That is, for the time in the air to double, the height of the jump must more than double. Some examples may be useful.

Let T be the total time during which there is no contact with the floor. Table 3.1 shows how much the height H of the jump changes for small changes in the timing. The strong dependence of the height of the jump on the time aloft is one of the main reasons dancers are acutely sensitive to slight changes in tempo. A tempo that slows by just 10 percent means a dancer would have to jump 21 percent higher to stay with the music, a difficult feat if the dancer is close to the limit of jump height.

Aha! Recall the conductor's comment in the anecdote at the beginning of this chapter. If the tempo of the music is slowed by the claimed 10 percent, you would have to jump not 10 percent higher, but 21 percent! That's why you were having trouble jumping high enough to stay with the music, and probably why you couldn't keep up with the music when it was faster—the effect of timing on jump height was again amplified, but in the opposite direction.

Of course, the message to the dancer is to control the timing of the jump *during the plié*, since the motion of the center of gravity in the air cannot be changed once contact with the ground is lost.

Now suppose the choreography and tempo of the music call for a series of vertical jumps that must be accomplished in 1/3 second each (not counting the time the feet are on the floor between jumps). The height of such jumps will be about 5 inches for *any* body. Suppose all dancers are told to point their feet during the jump and make sure the heels are on the floor between jumps (so as not to strain the Achilles tendon). Those with small feet can meet the challenge, because the height of the jump is sufficient to allow for a pointed foot with clearance above the floor. But the long-footed dancer is simply out of luck! There is no way he or she can point the feet in the time allowed. Increasing the height of the jump in order to provide clearance above the

Table 3.1 Vertical jump height versus time in the air

T (seconds)	1/4	1/3	1/2	1
H	3 in	5.5 in	1 ft	4 ft

floor extends the time of the jump, and the movement is no longer performed in tempo.

Recognize that some vertical jumps involve a change in body shape during the time in the air. For instance, the feet and legs can be raised relative to the rest of the body, as demonstrated by Benjamin Pierce in figure 3.6. If the center of gravity rises the same amount H for the same time in the air, the height of the feet above the floor can be significantly greater than H.

Connections between Horizontal and Vertical Motions

So far in this chapter we have looked at horizontal motions (accelerations from rest, slowing from forward motion, and traveling in a curved path) and vertical motions (jumps) separately. It is true that the two motions are separable for the purposes of physical analysis: horizontal forces produce horizontal accelerations and vertical forces produce vertical accelerations. But there are connections. Jumps combined with horizontal motions (such as *grands jetés*) produce trajectories, or paths of motion in space, which have certain well-known properties. It is also true that there are connections between vertical forces at the floor and the horizontal forces that result from friction. These friction forces would not exist without some vertical force pressing the foot against the floor.

A jump with horizontal motion can be higher than a vertical jump because of the transfer of some of the horizontal momentum to vertical momentum. (An extreme case of this transfer is seen in a pole-vaulter, who uses the flexible fiberglass pole to maximize the transfer of horizontal momentum to vertical.)

The Grand Jeté "Floating" Illusion

What is the shape of the trajectory in the air for the *grand jeté*, and what control does the dancer have over that trajectory? Once the body loses contact with the floor, the center of gravity will follow a parabolic trajectory—an arc—that is *totally determined* by the conditions of motion at the beginning of the trajectory. (The

FIGURE 3.6. Benjamin Pierce performing a vertical jump in which his legs, lifted relative to the rest of his body, can be higher off the ground for a similar rise in the center of gravity.

parabola is the particular shape of the curved path in space.) Although the dancer may change the shape and configuration of the body in flight (which can produce certain illusions), there is nothing the dancer can do to change the trajectory of the center of gravity until contact with the floor is reestablished. The trajectory will be a combination of a constant horizontal velocity and the vertical motion associated with a jump—a motion rising with a speed that decreases, goes to zero, then increases in the negative direction as the center of gravity descends. The time of flight is still given by table 3.1, which was developed for purely vertical motion.

An interesting illusion can be created by changing the body configuration during flight. One sometimes sees an impressive *grand jeté* in which the dancer seems to defy gravity by floating horizontally near the peak of the jump for a brief time before beginning the descent, rather than following the expected curved trajectory. This effect is partly due to the simple fact that the vertical motion of the body is rapid at the beginning and end of the jump but slow near the peak as the vertical speed slows to zero and reverses for descent. In fact, half of the total time the body is in the air is spent within one-quarter of the height from the peak. That is, if the center of gravity rises 2 feet during the *grand jeté*, the total time in the air is about 0.7 second, half of which, or 0.35 second, is spent within 6 inches of the peak. But the dancer can change body configuration in such a way that this floating illusion is even stronger.

Although the center of gravity follows a curved trajectory that is determined by the conditions of the initial takeoff from the floor, the position of the center of gravity *relative to the body* can be changed. Suppose the center of gravity when the dancer first leaves the floor is in the abdominal area, when the legs and arms are rather low. When the center of gravity has risen part way through its curved path through space, the arms and legs are raised, causing the center of gravity to move up in the body, perhaps to the stomach or above. If the timing is right, the center of gravity will continue to rise to the peak of the curved path, then begin to fall, while the torso and head of the body actually move horizontally. (See figure 3.7.) Since the eye of the observer is likely to follow the head and torso, an illusion is created that the dancer is actually floating horizontally for a few brief moments! A necessary component of the body movement that produces this illusion, then, is the raising of the legs, ideally to a "split," at the peak of the jump. Such a split is often seen in an impressive *grand jeté*, but it is now seen not only as an added stylistic flair unrelated to the shape of the jump itself, but as a component of the motion contributing directly to this illusion of "floating." But the split must be timed to coincide with the peak of the curved path of the body's center of gravity in order to produce the smoothest appearance of horizontal motion. The sequence of three instants in the *grand jeté* demonstrated by Sean in figure 3.8 shows many of these characteristics.

The Effect of Turnout on Traveling Jumps

Should a traveling jump such as a *grand jeté* be performed with the feet and legs turned out? The accepted aesthetic quality for essentially all *ballet* movements

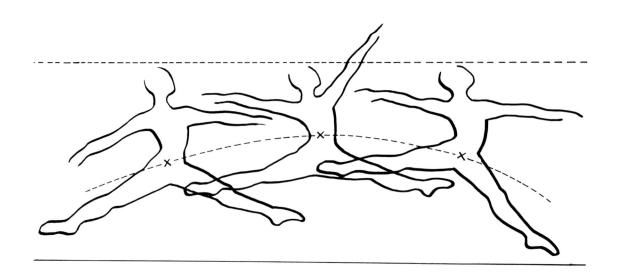

FIGURE 3.7.
The *grand jeté*
"floating" illu-
sion, in which the
center of gravity
follows a curved
(parabolic) trajec-
tory but moves
its position in the
body as the con-
figuration of the
body changes.

includes turnout. A *grand jeté* across the stage, however, represents one movement in which another important quality, the height of the jump, is sacrificed if the ideal degree of turnout is maintained. Compromise is clearly necessary, in which a choreographer's or teacher's judgment determines the quality more important for the immediate purpose.

Consider two extremes. In the first case the *grand jeté* is performed *en face*, moving directly to the dancer's left, with complete turnout, so that the right foot is pointed directly right as the push-off for the *grand jeté* to the left occurs. In the other extreme, the body is turned toward the direction of motion and turnout is totally sacrificed, so that the *glissade* becomes a running step to the left, with both feet pointed to the left, in the direction of motion. (See figure 3.9.)

The jump will be significantly stronger and higher in the latter case. The reason involves the angle through which the push-off foot moves while it extends in the ankle joint, allowing the foot to exert the force against the floor that results in an upward acceleration of the body. If the right foot is turned out, it is already partially extended at the beginning of the rise of the heel off the floor. The calf muscles then extend the foot, resulting in the force through the foot against the floor. As shown in the diagrams in figure 3.9, the angle through which the force can be exerted is thus less than 90°, from a partially extended position to a fully extended angle. However, when the foot is pointing in the direction of movement, it is flexed to an acute angle with the leg at the beginning of the jump, and thus can ideally extend through a change of significantly more than 90° to the fully extended position. When the force is exerted through a larger angle of travel of the foot, more momentum and energy are contributed to the jump. (The two approaches to the *jeté* are demonstrated by Sean in figure 3.10.)

We must realize that this is a simplified picture, as we have not taken into account the bending of the leg during takeoff. Both the straightening of the leg and the extending of the foot contribute to the force that provides the momentum for the jump. Also, in the dance movement described, one would never observe either extreme of turnout or turn-in discussed here. There is always some degree of compromise. But it is true that the human body is constructed such that our feet generally point in the direction of movement. This body configuration contributes to the effective use of the muscles in accomplishing the purpose of running or jumping.

Landings from Jumps

Now let us consider the sudden deceleration, or decrease in downward speed, that occurs as the body lands from a jump. Of course the foot will decelerate more rapidly than other parts of the body because it has no other springy part of the body to cushion its fall (extend its deceleration). The torso must decrease its downward velocity from the free-fall velocity to zero when landing, but the bending of the legs allows this velocity change to occur over a sizable distance (perhaps 1 foot) and an associated time of about 1/4 second. The landing foot and lower leg, however, must lose the same velocity of fall in a much shorter distance. Suppose the sole of a shoe and the padding of flesh between the skin and the bony structure of the foot can compress a total of 1/10 inch. For a jump in which the center of gravity has risen 2 feet, the downward velocity just before landing is about 11 feet per second. If that velocity changes to zero in a distance of 1/10 inch, the deceleration is about 240 times the acceleration due to gravity, or 240 g! Although the total mass of the foot that must be decelerated is small,

FIGURE 3.8. Sean Lavery's *grand jeté*, viewed clockwise, illustrating the illusion described in the accompanying analysis and shown in figure 3.7.

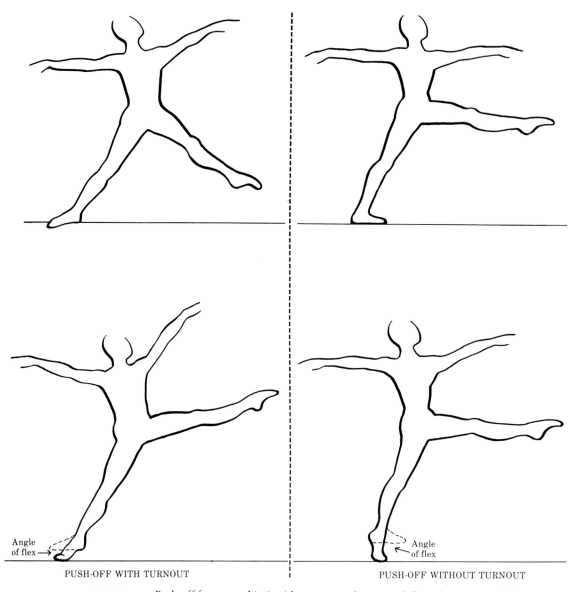

Angle
of flex →

PUSH-OFF WITH TURNOUT

Angle
of flex

PUSH-OFF WITHOUT TURNOUT

FIGURE 3.9. Push-off for a *grand jeté*, with exaggerated turnout (left) and no turnout (right).

FIGURE 3.10.
Sean Lavery pushing off
for a *grand jeté* with
turnout (top) and with-
out (bottom), as shown
in figure 3.9.

55

that deceleration can be potentially harmful. One of the skills dancers learn in order to protect the feet from such decelerations is to decrease the speed of descent of the feet just before landing. That is, the feet begin to move upward relative to the center of gravity of the body just before landing, thereby cushioning the impact of the feet on the floor.

Dancers are sometimes called upon to fall to the floor rather than only land on their feet from jumps. Again, the decelerating forces can be large, depending on what part of the body strikes the ground first, and with what vertical velocity. If the hands are used to break a fall, the same analysis as applied above for the feet can be used to analyze the effect on the hands. Of course if much of the weight of the falling body is subsequently borne by the hands, the continued stress can cause problems and perhaps injury. In the next section we will see how the nature of the floor can have a major impact on the body's reaction to landings or falls.

Dance Floors: Elasticity and Friction

Note that the horizontal accelerations discussed earlier depend on friction between the feet and the floor. And the effectiveness and safety of vertical jumps depend on the quality of the floor—the amount of "spring" in the floor. Both the elastic properties and the surface friction are often inadequate for the demands placed on them by dancers. Let us analyze those two characteristics of floors.

First, let us consider the vertical elastic property of a floor, which is important for a safe landing. Elasticity involves both large-scale "springiness" and small-scale "rubberiness." Does a springy floor aid in the jumping process as a diving board would, or does it allow higher jumps only because of the psychological effect of an anticipated cushioned landing? Actually, the magnitude of vertical motion in a springy floor is rather small—less than an inch—while the vertical displacement of the body's center of gravity during the push-off for a jump is at least a foot. This implies that the contribution of the floor to the magnitude of vertical velocity at the end of the push-off is rather small.

Let us return to the deceleration experienced by the foot upon descent and landing from a jump. If the padding provided by the shoe and the sole of the foot allows a compression of 1/10 inch, then the deceleration upon landing is about 240 g. But if the floor adds additional vertical motion of 1 inch, the deceleration is only about one-tenth as great. Thus, the "give" in the floor, probably insignificant in increasing the height of a jump directly, results in a large decrease in the potentially dangerous deceleration of the body upon landing.

This principle is very evident in some easily observed situations. The air bags used by high jumpers and pole-vaulters for their landings extend the time and vertical distance over which the free-fall velocity may be decreased to zero. An automobile bumper with some spring to it will cause and sustain less damage than a stiff one. Closer to home, there is less discomfort when one trips and falls if the landing is made on the padded buttocks rather than the unpadded head!

Now what benefit is gained from the use of linoleum or rubber-like stage floors commonly used for dance? Two important properties are the controlled uniformity and sound-deadening capability. Many stages have holes, grooves, slippery spots, and other problems that can be covered by a portable dance floor. And the sound of a hard shoe surface (such as the toe of a *pointe* shoe) striking a floor can be decreased substantially by even a small amount of small-scale elasticity. But it is also true that this small-scale "give" in a floor increases the area of contact between the toe of a *pointe* shoe and the floor. On a hard surface the curved toe will ride on the floor with only a very small part of the convex surface making contact. That small part will, of course, have an extremely large pressure due to the body weight and will wear rapidly. A slightly elastic floor surface will allow the shoe to sink into the surface a small amount, allowing a larger area of contact. Not only should this be easier on the shoe, but dancers claim they benefit from a greater "feel" of the floor.

Now we return to a traveling jump such as the *grand jeté* and dancers' common concern about the potential slipperiness of a floor. Is rosin on the floor always the appropriate solution? What are the principles involved in the frictional properties of floors?

Friction involves the properties of the surfaces in contact, both chemical and mechanical. Both chemical adhesion between surfaces and microscopic roughness contribute to a frictional force that acts in a direction along the interface between the surfaces. For many pairs of interacting surfaces the magnitude of the friction force is proportional to the perpendicular force pressing the two surfaces together. The constant of proportionality is called the coefficient of friction.

Rosin is sometimes used on a floor to increase friction. Whether a dancer needs a change in linear horizontal motion or a rotational acceleration, the floor must be able to supply the horizontal forces that provide for such accelerations. The perpendicular (vertical) force is equal to the person's weight if there are no vertical accelerations, so the only way to increase friction is to change the nature of the surfaces.

Many dance movements involve sliding on the floor or rotating on a pivoting supporting foot. Too much friction will inhibit these movements, which may include *glissades* and *assemblés* in addition to all types of *pirouettes*. But insufficient friction allows the feet to slip when such loss of equilibrium can be disastrous. The portable dance floor coverings often used on stage and studio floors have the frictional properties dancers need: enough friction to stick when sticking is needed and little enough friction to allow for turns and glides.

When such floors are not available, rosin is often used. One characteristic of rosin is that it has a large static coefficient of friction and a significantly smaller dynamic coefficient. That is, if the foot is stationary on the floor, a large horizontal frictional force is possible, but if the foot is moving, that force is substantially smaller. That difference is very useful to a dancer, who needs the horizontal force only when the foot is not moving against the floor. (That difference is also the reason rosin is used on bows for stringed instruments, for which a stick-slip-stick-slip process is responsible for the resonant oscillation produced by the bow on the string.)

Why don't modern dancers, who perform many of the same sorts of movements as ballet dancers, use rosin? Modern dance is usually performed in bare feet. Since the skin is usually somewhat moist (particularly when the body is exercising), the characteristics of the surfaces in contact are different than when dry. A small amount of moisture makes surfaces in contact less slippery; too much moisture reverses that effect, since there can now be a film of water between the surfaces. The normal skin moisture is appropriate for the movements of a modern dancer, whereas rosin adds more friction than the bare feet can withstand, giving rise to blisters or worse. Ballet dancers often use a little water on the floor or the shoes to provide a degree of friction similar to that of moist bare feet.

A Final Leap

A dancer performing linear movements—vertical, horizontal, or a combination—must control the forces exerted against the floor. These forces are responsible for the accelerations, or changes in the state of motion. Horizontal acceleration from rest requires a horizontal force against the floor. This force can arise from a shift in the center of supporting force relative to the center of gravity of the body, or from an acceleration of part of the body, such as a leg in a *tombé*.

Motion in a horizontal curved path requires an acceleration, in this case because of the change in *direction* of the velocity. That acceleration requires a horizontal force directed toward the center of the curved path, a force that can only come from the floor, and must be accompanied by a lean toward the center of curvature, as in a banked curve on a road. The faster the motion, or the tighter the turn, the greater the lean from vertical. Friction against the floor is often the limiting factor in establishing how fast or tight the curved path can be.

Horizontal motion can be stopped only if there is a horizontal force against the floor in the direction of motion (resulting in a force from the floor on the body in a direction such as to oppose the motion). A landing from a traveling jump has to be made with the center of gravity behind the landing foot in order to allow the body to coast to a stop in a stable position.

Vertical jumps require vertical forces against the floor that must be adjusted to produce the height required and the time in the air determined by the rhythm of the music. The relationship between height and duration is fixed by nature and is independent of body size. It takes a jump four times as high to last twice as long. If the arms are moved upward during the take-off phase of the jump, the height can be increased substantially—about 25 percent.

In-flight trajectories, involving combined vertical and horizontal motions, always have a parabolic shape for the path of the center of gravity. Nothing a dancer does after take-off from the floor can change the trajectory of the center of gravity. The horizontal component of motion in the trajectory is always a straight line while the body is in the air. The vertical component of motion is identical to that in a vertical jump. The illusion of "floating," or temporarily stopping the downward acceleration at the peak of the jump, is accomplished by shifting the vertical position of the center of gravity in the body so that the torso and head move only horizontally for a short time near the peak of the jump while the center of gravity continues its curved trajectory.

The vertical impulse that can be produced for a traveling jump depends on the range of motion of the foot around the ankle pivot. That range of motion is limited when turnout is maintained, and the height of a jump is sacrificed.

Both elastic and frictional properties of dance floors are important for dancers, the former for vertical motions and the latter for horizontal accelerations. Elasticity contributes little to the vertical impulse in a jump, but does allow a softer landing that decreases the potential for injury. Rosin is used on inadequate floors in order to increase friction of the feet against the floor because it tends to be "sticky" when there is *no* motion but allows motion more easily once the feet are moving on the floor. Thus, *glissades* and *pirouettes* are possible at the same time that there is sufficient friction to allow for rapid accelerations or decelerations.

Dancers are well aware of the dangers involved in large movements on stage. Probably every dancer has experienced the embarrassment of a fall. When one recognizes the forces between the feet and the floor that are necessary in order to carry out the movements observed, it may be a wonder that these movements are possible at all! Just the inward lean of the body during a circular movement around the stage invites a slip and fall. And the forces required for the high leaps, particularly in the landings that are most likely to produce injuries, can be enormous. But there is no way of avoiding these forces if dancers are to display the full range of movements expected of them. The audience, and the art of dance, are well served by these efforts on the part of dancers!

4   PIROUETTES

The choreographer has just asked you to do a sixteen-turn *pirouette* at a constant tempo! After you realize that he's serious, your mind starts racing. Of course, you know that you would constantly lose momentum due to friction while turning, and you would not be able to maintain balance for so long. But then an idea comes to you, and you answer the choreographer, "OK, I can do that!"

What would you have in mind to meet such a challenge?

Turning movements are common in all forms of dance. One of the most common is the *pirouette*, or rotation of the body around a vertical axis over one supporting foot on the floor. There are many types and styles of *pirouettes*, from a low turn on bent leg in modern dance to the impressive multiple *fouetté* turns or *grandes pirouettes* often seen in the classical ballet repertoire. There are "pencil turns," *attitude* or *arabesque* turns, and "illusion turns" in addition to the standard vertical *pirouettes*. Most turns can be performed in either direction on either supporting leg. The various turns have both common aspects and uniquely different characteristics and problems.

Brief descriptions of these turns will be useful:

- An *en dedans* turn is any *pirouette* toward the supporting leg (a right turn on the right supporting leg, for instance). In the normal *pirouette* position in ballet, the supporting leg is straight and almost vertical, and the "gesture" leg (or "working" leg) is raised to the side with the foot at the knee of the supporting leg (sometimes called a *retiré* position).
- An *en dehors* turn is *away* from the supporting leg.
- *Attitude* turns can be *en dedans* or *en dehors*, *en avant* or *derrière* (depending on whether the bent leg is in front of or behind the body).
- An *arabesque* turn is an *en dedans pirouette* with one leg extended to the rear in *arabesque* position.
- An "illusion turn" is a turn with the body, except for the supporting leg, inverted.
- A *grande pirouette* is a turn with the leg extended horizontally to the side (*à la seconde*).
- *Fouetté* turns are repeated *pirouettes en dehors* with the gesture leg extended away from the body during a part of each turn.

In this chapter we will look at the mechanisms used for initiating a *pirouette*, which involve forces acting from outside the body to cause the body to start turning. We will look at the powerful concept of rotational momentum. The principle of

FIGURE 4.1. A rotating dancer stopped by the camera during a *pirouette*. Martha Swope/ TimePix.

conservation of rotational momentum allows us to understand what changes are possible when the horizontal forces acting on the body are so small that the rotational momentum is effectively constant.

We will then examine some specific *pirouette* movements that demonstrate intriguing applications of physical principles that determine the shape and appearance of the movements. *Pirouettes* performed with the help of a partner will be discussed in chapter 7.

Torque and Rotational Momentum in a Pirouette

If a body is initially at rest, and a short time later is moving as a whole, some inter-action with the world outside the body is necessary. In the same way that a force acting on a body at rest causes it to start moving in some direction, a body is caused to rotate by a torque applied to it. In general, a body can move as a whole in some direction *and* rotate simultaneously. But that complex situation will be investigated in the next chapter; here we will deal with pure rotations, or turns that leave the body's center of gravity essentially fixed in location.

A torque can be thought of as a kind of force that causes a rotation, like the hand turning a screwdriver or two hands turning a T-shaped wrench to tighten bolts on a car wheel. Such a torque is actually a combination of at least one pair of forces (called a force couple) acting on a body in opposite directions, with some distance between the lines along which the forces act. Widely separated forces acting on a body produce more torque and thus are more effective in producing rotations than forces acting close together. For instance, it is harder to tighten bolts with thin-handled screw-drivers and short-handled wrenches than with thick- or long-handled ones.

Consider a dancer starting a *pirouette* from a fourth-position preparation, with one foot some distance behind the other on the floor. When the turn is started, the dancer pushes sideways in opposite directions with the two feet, as shown in figures 4.2 and 4.3. The result of the forces of the floor acting on the feet (associated with the forces exerted by the feet against the floor) is to create a torque that starts the body rotating. If the feet are very close together, as in a fifth-position preparation with one foot immediately behind and touching the other and pointed in the oppo-site direction, the torque is smaller. It is harder to initiate the turn, just as it is harder to tighten a bolt with a short-handled wrench or open a door by pushing near the hinged edge. Requiring even more force, and therefore more difficult, is a turn in which the torque is exerted by just the supporting foot while it is flat on the floor. In that case, the front of the foot pushes one sideways direction, and the back of the foot the other. (Experiments have shown that, as expected because of the direction of necessary twist of the foot, this "single-foot torque" is possible only with *pirou-*

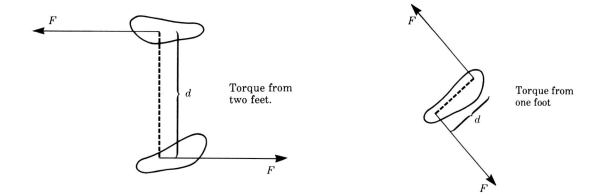

Torque from two feet.

Torque from one foot

ettes en dedans.) In any case, the possibility of any significant torque being applied to the body effectively ends when the supporting foot rises onto *pointe* or *demi-pointe*, and the size of the contact area becomes very small.

Rotational momentum is a "quantity" of rotational motion. The total rotational momentum L of a body can change only if there is an external torque acting on the body. There is no way that changes in body position alone—changes in the configuration of mass within the rotating system—can change the total L. It is sometimes claimed that "spotting" the head one more time can squeeze an extra turn out of a multiple *pirouette*. ("Spotting" is keeping the head fixed in direction while the remainder of the body turns, then rotating the head quickly around to face the original direction again.) But rotating the head relative to the rest of the body does not change the total L of the body as a whole, and hence cannot contribute any extra turning motion. One may feel as if the extra turn is there, but the additional rotation of the head only gives the *appearance* of a full additional turn. Then why do dancers spot? Apparently, spotting prevents dizziness by providing a fixed focus for the eyes and a nonrotating head for part of the movement.

What determines how much rotational momentum L a dancer can acquire in a *pirouette*? The dancer's feet, assumed to start in the fourth-position preparation described above, push sideways against the floor in opposite directions in order to produce the torque that starts the turn. The total L acquired in that process is determined by the size of the torque exerted on the body *and* by the length of time

FIGURE 4.2. Force couples (F) and torques between the feet and the floor, which produce the turning motion for *pirouettes.*

FIGURE 4.3.
Narrow and wide fourth-position preparations for a *pirouette en dehors*. The wide fourth position, with the larger distance between the forces, requires less horizontal force between the feet and the floor to produce the same torque.

that torque is applied. Now what happens as the turning motion begins? If the direction the body faces changes quickly at the beginning of the turn so that it is impossible to continue exerting those forces, then the final L will be limited. But if there is some way of storing the L acquired during the push so that the body can remain in its initial orientation, then the length of time the torque can be exerted on the body can be increased, resulting in a greater accumulated total rotational momentum. How does the dancer accomplish this storing of L? One technique is often seen, particularly when *pirouettes* are performed from fifth position, for which the distance between the lines of action of the forces at the feet, and hence the resulting torque, is small. The arms are observed to "wind up," or start rotating before the rest of the body does. Those arms are thus storing rotational momentum that is eventually transferred back to the body as a whole, allowing for a greater rate of turn.

Although a greater turn rate can be achieved by means of the "windup," dancers are usually admonished not to employ it, or at least to minimize it. This is an example in which use of the physical principle that makes a movement easier is counterproductive in achieving the desired aesthetic image, since most teachers, choreographers, and dancers feel that the appearance of the turn is compromised by thewindup. Maximizing the rate of turn is not considered as important as other visible aspects of the movement, although most dancers, if asked to perform a large number of turns in a *pirouette*, will knowingly employ a windup.

Controlling Rotational Velocity

The feeling and appearance of a *pirouette* are directly related to the turn rate. How is that turn rate related to the total rotational momentum L? The momentum is greater if the rate of turn (number of revolutions per second) is greater *or* if the mass of the body is distributed farther from the rotation axis. Mathematically,

$$L = I\omega$$

where I is the rotational inertia, which is the quantity that increases when mass is farther from the rotation axis, and ω (lowercase Greek omega) is the rate of turn. So for a given rate of turn, a dancer's L is greater when the legs and arms are extended to the side than when they are close to the body. And, for a constant body configuration, L is greater the more rapid the turn.

The important thing about rotational momentum is that it is a quantity that remains constant when no torques act on the body. In that case, a change in the distance of body mass from the rotation axis will produce a change in the rate of turn. That is, if the arms or legs are brought closer to the body, then the rate of turn *increases*, assuming there is little friction at the floor, which would tend to decrease the total L. (If one of the quantities in the above equation for L decreases, the other must increase to keep the product the same.)

Suppose a dancer is performing a *pirouette* with leg in *retiré* (foot at the knee of the supporting leg) and arms extended to the front, and then lowers the arms and lifted leg, bringing them closer to the axis of rotation. The speed of the turn will tend to increase. Of course, there is friction between the foot and the floor, so L will actually be decreasing. But as the distribution of body mass changes, the expected decrease in turn rate due to friction can be partially offset, making the turn appear to continue at a constant rate longer than if the body were kept in a constant position. That phenomenon is quite evident in Mikhail Baryshnikov's eleven-turn *pirouette* in the movie *White Nights*.

When learning *pirouettes*, one sometimes hears the instruction to "go up and then turn." Since the rotational momentum L is constant after the accelerating torque ceases, this instruction seems impossible. However, the arms are often extended during the accelerating phase of the turn, so the rate of turn is not very large while L is increasing to its maximum. Then when the arms are brought in closer to the body, the turn rate increases, thus creating the illusion of turning only after rising onto the supporting foot. In the case of the *arabesque* turn or the *grande pirouette*, the body remains extended, so the rate of turn never becomes very large. (But that turn rate increases near the end of the turn if the working leg is finally brought in to the normal *pirouette* position for the last few rapid turns.)

How does friction slow the *pirouette*, limiting the number of turns possible? When a dancer is *en pointe*, the area of supporting contact with the floor is very small. We have seen how this affects conditions of balance. It is also true that there is less retarding torque for *pirouettes* performed *en pointe*. The perpendicular force holding the foot and the floor together is still just the dancer's weight, so the horizontal friction forces are the same. But the torque resulting from those forces depends on the distance from their lines of action to the rotation axis. If the area of support is small, the friction forces act very close to the axis of rotation, so the resulting retarding torque is small.

When the turn is to be stopped, the foot (or feet) return flat to the floor, allowing the retarding friction to increase, and the arms are extended, which slows the rotational velocity for the rotational momentum remaining. Coordinating these two actions of the body allows the turn to end in the desired orientation.

Characteristics of Pirouettes

Let us look at some of the differences between types of turns. Most of the examples will be from the classical ballet vocabulary, but the results may be generalized to other forms of turns around a vertical axis on one supporting foot. Recall the *en dehors* and *en dedans pirouettes*, *arabesque* and *attitude* turns, *grandes pirouettes*, and *fouetté* turns described earlier.

Experiments have shown that the total rotational momentum is significantly less for *pirouettes en pointe* than on *demi-pointe*, least for *pirouettes en dehors* and greatest (about 30 percent larger) for *arabesque* turns.[1] The latter is interesting in that the rate of turn is faster (more than double) for the *pirouette en dehors* than for the *arabesque* turn. Clearly, the distance of body mass from the rotation axis makes the difference, being substantially greater for the *arabesque* turn with extended leg. So even though a greater L is achieved for such a turn, requiring a greater initiating torque, the turn rate is small because of the extended body configuration.

1. Kenneth Laws, "An Analysis of Turns in Dance," *Dance Research Journal* 11, nos. 1–2 (1978–79).

The same experiments mentioned above also showed that spotting the head during the turn (turning the head quickly from front around to front again) occupies about half of the total time of the turn for a *pirouette en dehors*. For the slower turns, the head often just turns with the rest of the body.

The Arabesque *Turn*

An *arabesque* turn in classical ballet, an *en dedans pirouette* with one leg extended to the back of the dancer, is a beautiful movement when performed well. But there is a common difficulty one can observe in students learning the movement or in dancers lacking the requisite proficiency. And there is an interesting physical reason behind this prevalent problem.

The *arabesque* turn requires exerting a torque with the two feet on the floor, then lifting the push-off leg into a horizontal position to the rear. After the leg reaches the horizontal position, there is a strong tendency for it to drop back down, as in a *grand battement derrière*, or kicking movement to the rear. (See figure 4.4.) When the leg is fully extended horizontally, a substantial part of the body mass is far from the rotation axis, which makes the rate of turn small for the magnitude of *L* generated from the initial torque. When the leg drops, its mass is not as far from the axis of rotation, so the turn rate increases, making the turn seem easier, faster, and more satisfying. The drooping leg, since it is behind the body, is not easily seen by the dancer (except in the wall mirror often present in ballet classes).

An interesting phenomenon now occurs. Since the turn rate has increased, there is an increased centrifugal force tending to throw the leg away from the axis of rotation out toward horizontal again! The resulting decreased turn rate then allows the leg again to descend, and the process may repeat. So a dancer may experience an oscillation of the leg up to the horizontal, down, then up again, possibly repeated for a multiple *arabesque* turn. (See figure 4.5.) Such an oscillation can be observed in dancers who do not emphasize keeping the leg fixed in the *arabesque* position with the help of their proprioceptive senses—the internal senses the mind uses to determine body positions without visual cues.

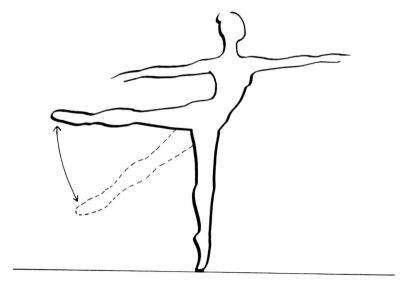

FIGURE 4.4. "Drooping" leg in an *arabesque* turn.

Is this oscillating-leg syndrome bad? Perhaps the choreographer intends such a movement. But the traditional *arabesque* turn in ballet, which is a common and impressive movement, is done ideally with the gesture leg fixed in a horizontal position. Choreographers do sometimes depart from the ideal for artistic reasons, and similar turns in other styles of dance may depart in specific details from the classical ballet model.

Lisa de Ribère performed the *arabesque* turn with the "drooping leg" for the camera in order to illustrate the problem. The resulting sequence of photographs is shown in figure 4.5.

At what frequency might the gesture leg be oscillating up and down? The problem is not a simple one, because the centrifugal effect, the position of the leg, and the turn rate are all connected. The results of the analysis described in appendix G show that, for a typical body shape and turn rate, the leg's oscillation frequency is very close to the rotation frequency. That is, for a rotation rate of one full turn in 1 second, the leg may oscillate up and down at the same rate; that is, once each revolution. This "resonance" between the two frequencies may make it particularly difficult to overcome the problem, since the natural frequency of the oscillation of

FIGURE 4.5. Sequence of five consecutive instants in an *arabesque* turn, demonstrating the drooping-leg problem (clockwise from top). The gesture leg oscillates down and up about once during the complete turn shown.

the leg is synchronized with the rotation! The good *arabesque* position would occur when the body is facing one side, when the *arabesque* line is most effectively displayed for the audience, then occur again when the body returns to that orientation. In between, the dancer rotates rapidly when the leg is lower. The movement may thus have its own appeal, but it does not maintain the shape of the *arabesque* expected in the *arabesque* turn.

The "Illusion Turn"

The "illusion turn," a *pirouette* often seen in jazz dance and other forms of movement, including ice skating, can be analyzed using some of the same ideas used in the arabesque turn analysis. This turn, an *en dedans* turn (toward the supporting leg), starts with a push-off from the left leg onto the right, supporting leg. But after the turn is started, the torso and arms drop to an upside-down position with the left leg rising up to be close to vertical. The turn ends with the left leg returning toward the floor, the torso rising back up to its normal vertical position.

As the left leg and torso approach their inverted positions, they are temporarily extended away from the vertical rotation axis, thereby slowing the rotation. Then when they reach their inverted positions, they are closer to the axis, allowing the turn rate to increase substantially. But then the effective centrifugal force comes into play, tending to throw the torso and left leg away from the axis and back toward the horizontal, thus slowing the turn rate again. The turn ends smoothly as the body again approaches an upright position with the mass close to the axis as the rotational momentum is decreasing, preventing the movement from ending abruptly after the torso and leg are no longer horizontal.

The time shape of this movement is therefore: start; slow a bit briefly; whip around quickly while inverted; slow again coming out of the inverted position; coast to a stop in an upright position. That characteristic movement shape is a direct result of the changes in mass distribution relative to the rotation axis, with the resulting changes in turn rate for a total rotational momentum that slowly decreases due to friction.

The Grande Pirouette

Another interesting effect occurs in a *grande pirouette* and also in other turns with a straight, extended gesture leg, such as the *arabesque* turn described earlier. Since the body position for the *grande pirouette* is identical to a stationary pose often seen— the body *en face* with the gesture leg horizontal to the side *à la seconde*—one might wonder if the condition for balance is the same whether the body is rotating or not. The physical analysis of the condition for balance for a static body is straightforward, involving the masses, lengths, and positions of the various body segments. As shown in the top photograph in figure 4.6, the supporting leg is not quite vertical because of the amount of weight that is extended to the other side. For typical body segment masses and lengths, one can calculate the angle between the supporting leg and the vertical. This angle is about 4.5° for a male dancer. (The *grande pirouette* is most often performed in ballet by male dancers.)

Now suppose the body is rotating about a vertical axis through the supporting foot, as shown in the bottom photograph in figure 4.6. If the supporting leg again makes an angle of 4.5°, will the body be in balance while rotating? Strangely enough, no! The analysis is complicated and is described in appendix H. Briefly, it involves the following: Since the body position for the *grande pirouette* is not bilaterally symmetric (the right and left sides of the body have different configurations), the rotational momentum vector must precess around the vertical axis, as with a spinning top that is wobbling. That precession of L, necessary for a balanced turn, requires an angle between the supporting leg and the vertical that is less than the static 4.4°—in fact, about 3.5° for the same body data used to determine the static equilibrium. Although this difference in balance angle is small, and variations in the performance of the movements may be large enough to mask the effect, the photographs of Sean Lavery in figure 4.6 do seem to show a slight difference in angle, and he reported that he could feel the difference. Good dancers must be sensitive to very small shifts in position in order to achieve the remarkable feats of balance sometimes observed. Without a sensitivity to this shift in balance when the body is rotating, it is difficult to carry out the movement well.

FIGURE 4.6.
Sean Lavery in second
position, stationary (top)
and turning (bottom). The
condition for balance is
slightly different in the two
cases, with the supporting
leg closer to vertical when
the body is rotating.

The magnitude of that challenge is one reason the movement is impressive and rarely performed well.

Fouetté *Turns*

Fouetté turns are repeated *pirouettes* which begin as a normal *pirouette en dehors* but include a movement that allows the rotational momentum lost to friction to be regained once each revolution. Properly done *fouetté* turns are an impressive *"tour de force"* in a ballerina's vocabulary. One of the best-known examples in standard classical choreography is the thirty-two continuous *fouetté* turns by the Black Swan in act 3 of *Swan Lake*.

This turn is one of the few continuing turns, a fact that immediately suggests the question "How does the dancer maintain balance for an extended time while replacing rotational momentum lost because of friction?" The turn itself is a series of repeated *pirouettes* with a pause in the turn after each full rotation. (The sequence of photographs in figure 4.7 shows Lisa in various stages of a *fouetté* turn. A clockwise path through the six pictures shows the stages of the movement in proper order, and may be continued for the repeated turns.) While the body is turning, it is in a normal *pirouette* position, with the arms forming a circle to the front and the raised leg to the side with the foot at the knee of the supporting leg. When the torso and head are facing front, the leg is extended to the front, the arms start to open, and the supporting leg is bent slightly, with the heel down. As the raised leg moves from front to side it absorbs the rotational momentum of the turn while the torso, head, and arms remain facing the audience.

As the leg is brought back to the knee of the supporting leg, and the dancer rises again onto straight leg and pointed foot, the whole body again turns through a complete revolution since the rotational momentum now resides in the entire rotating body. The period of time during which the dancer's body is not rotating (less than half a second) provides an opportunity for regaining balance and exerting some torque against the floor with the flat supporting foot, thus regaining any

FIGURE 4.7. Lisa de Ribère performing *fouetté* turns. The sequence should be viewed clockwise, from the top, repetitively through the six frames. Note that the body rotates very little while the leg has most of the rotational momentum in views 2, 3, and 4. Then the body turns rapidly in 5 and 6 while the leg is held in a position close to the body, where it has less rotational inertia.

momentum lost by friction. Regaining balance is facilitated by the dancer's extending her arms to the sides, where they have a large inertia; a tightrope walker carries a long pole for the same reason. That large inertia allows for a larger sideways force against the floor when the same mechanism is employed for regaining balance as that used when the body is not rotating (discussed in chapter 2).

What characteristics of this movement can be changed by a choreographer or a dancer without destroying the movement itself? What characteristics are dictated by physical principles, and which are determined by aesthetic considerations? An important aspect of the turn is the motion of the leg from front to side while the rest of the body is temporarily stationary. In the Russian style of the *fouetté* turn, however, the leg is thrust directly to the side, which of course slows the rotation because of the increase in distance of body mass from the rotation axis, but does not allow the torso, head, and arms to stop briefly. In both styles, it is necessary to have the leg extended as far from the rotation axis of the body as possible in order for it to absorb the total rotational momentum of the turn without acquiring too large a rotation rate itself or, in the Russian style, to maximize the distance of the leg's mass from the axis of rotation so as to slow the body's turn rate as much as possible during that phase of the movement.

Quantitative calculations have been made using data on weights and dimensions of body segments for an average female dancer and a model of body positions for a good *fouetté* turn. Suppose a dancer is doing a normal *pirouette* at a rotation rate of two revolutions per second. When the body is facing front, the raised leg is extended forward and begins rotating to the side while the remainder of the body remains nonrotating. If the total rotational momentum L remains approximately constant during this entire turning cycle, then the turn rate is small when a significant mass of the body is far from the rotation axis. The calculations described in appendix I show that the rotation rate of the extended leg is only about one-half revolution per second when the rest of the body is not rotating. The movement of the leg from front to side (one-quarter turn) thus takes about 1/2 second, long enough for the dancer to regain balance and exert some torque with the supporting foot. This stationary phase of the total movement takes about half of the total time for a complete cycle of the motion, while the full-turn rotation of the body takes place in the remaining half.

Perhaps *fouetté* turns are the movement you had in mind when you told the choreographer that you could do a sixteen-turn *pirouette* at a constant tempo. You realized that you could keep the turn going by storing rotational momentum temporarily in the working leg while you come down onto the flat supporting foot in order to exert the torque that allows you to regain the rotational momentum lost to friction in the preceding turn. And you can use that brief pause to regain your balance if you feel that you are starting to topple.

Repeated Pirouettes

An analysis similar to that for *fouetté* turns applies to another repetitive turn—repeated *pirouettes* from fifth position. These are often *en dehors* turns (away from the supporting leg), with the body descending off *pointe* or *demi-pointe* into *demi-plié* with both feet down once each revolution when the body is *en face*. Again there must be a mechanism for the body to exert a torque against the floor in order to regain the small amount of rotational momentum lost to friction during the turn. This torque can most effectively be exerted by the feet against the floor if the body is temporarily stationary. The means of stopping the body is similar to that for the *fouetté* turn, but in this case the *arms*, rather than the gesture leg, rotate while the body stops. When the body reaches a position facing front, the lead arm and then the trailing arm rotate toward the turn, thus temporarily absorbing the rotational momentum and allowing the feet to perform their torque-exerting function. When the body returns to the *pirouette* position, the arms transfer the rotational momentum back to the body as a whole.

Since in this movement the arms, being lighter and shorter than a leg, are less effective than the gesture leg in the *fouetté* turn, the effect is less noticeable, and the repeated turns do seem to be more continuous. In fact, using the anatomical data and techniques developed in the appendixes, the two arms together are only about one-third as effective as one leg. But the fundamental mechanical process is the same.

Another example of a turn in which the same effect can be detected is the *grande pirouette* discussed earlier in this chapter. This turn usually includes a return to a flat supporting foot and *demi-plié* once each revolution. In this case some torque is exerted by the supporting foot against the floor during the time the foot is flat rather than on *pointe* or *demi-pointe*. Again this torque can be exerted more effectively if most of the body is temporarily slowed, if not stopped, in its rotation. The gesture leg does swing a small amount in the horizontal plane during that *en face* moment, and the arms may help some, too. The effect is less pronounced than for the previously described turns, but a good dancer will adjust body position somewhat to make the movement as smooth as possible by controlling where the rotational momentum resides during different phases of the turn.

Other repeating turns include the traveling *piqué* turns shown in figure 4.8. Each turn on one leg is followed by a traveling step to the other leg, then back to the first for another turn. They can be performed in either direction of rotation, on either leg.

A Final Turn

All of the turns discussed in this chapter have common characteristics involving the preparation, the mechanisms for developing the torque to initiate or maintain the turn, and the control of the body's mass distribution to determine the rate of turn. Some repeated turns involve, in addition, transfers of rotational momentum from one part of the body to another, a process that provides a more effective means of gaining momentum from a torque against the floor while the body is rotating.

All turning movements require a torque to create the rotational momentum needed. For solo *pirouettes*, the torque comes from a force couple exerted by the feet against the floor. The larger the distance between the lines of action of the two forces making up the force couple, the greater the torque. Thus a *pirouette* preparation position in which the feet are spread far apart allows the forces at the feet to be more effective in producing the accelerating torque. *Pirouettes* from fifth position, as well as *pirouettes* in which the torque comes largely from just one foot in

FIGURE 4.8. New York City Ballet dancers performing *piqué* turns in George Balanchine's *Serenade*.

contact with the floor, are more difficult because the separation of the forces is small. *Pirouettes en dehors* are initiated by torques exerted only while *both* feet are on the ground; the torque for *en dedans* turns can involve some contribution from the supporting foot after the push-off foot has left the floor. The "single-foot" torque is not effective for *en dehors* turns because the direction of twist of the foot would be toward greater turnout of the supporting leg, which is difficult if the dancer is already maximally turned out.

In starting a turn, it is usually effective, although not always aesthetically acceptable, to rotate the arms in the direction of the turn while the torque is being exerted against the floor. In this "windup," the arms absorb much of the rotational momentum while the body is in a position that makes possible the effective use of the feet for continuing to exert torque.

Controlling the turn rate after rising onto *pointe* or *demi-pointe* requires controlling the distribution of body mass relative to the rotation axis. The farther the body mass is from the axis, the slower the rate of turn. This fact explains why a *grande pirouette* speeds up when the arms and legs are brought closer to the body. It also explains the mechanism for a *pirouette en dedans* when started with a *degagé seconde*, which delays the turn of the torso at the beginning while that gesture leg is storing momentum to be transferred to the rest of the body a short time later.

Arabesque turns are slower because of the amount of body mass that is far from the axis of rotation. And they are often flawed by a raised leg that oscillates up and down during the turn. This oscillation is a natural phenomenon that can, in fact, have the same timing as the period of rotation, making the problem particularly insidious. The placement of the body and the strength with which the leg is held in position are extremely important in maintaining the horizontal *arabesque* line during this turn.

The *grande pirouette* requires a balance position slightly different than the position of condition for the same position without the rotation. The effect of the turn is to require the supporting leg to lean a bit less away from the vertical than it does for the nonrotating case.

Fouetté turns are characterized by a temporary pause in the rotation once each revolution when the dancer is facing the audience. That pause is made possible by the transfer of rotational momentum L from the whole body to the raised leg, which rotates from front to side while the rest of the body remains facing front. That rotation of the gesture leg is therefore an important characteristic of the *fouetté* turn. Repeated *pirouettes* from fifth position involve a transfer of L that is more subtle but is based on the same principle. In this case the L is transferred to the arms, which temporarily rotate relative to the rest of the body while the dancer is facing front.

To what extent are dancers aware of the physical principles that govern the way rotations occur? As in many other cases, but particularly for the subtleties of rotational motion, dancers have learned exactly how to perform the movements by experience, instruction, trial and error, and observing others. It is a wonder that dancers achieve the desired results so effectively, in ways that unconsciously use these mechanical principles that are usually applied to wheels, gyroscopes, and planets.

5 TURNS
in the air

You know that in tomorrow's performance you're supposed to nail that double *tour en l'air* (a vertical jump with two full turns in the air)—and you still can only get around one and a half turns. And that looks sloppy! At least for the preparation you are keeping your feet in a good tight fifth position (feet touching each other, toe to heel and heel to toe) in order to keep your rotational inertia small when you turn. Others aren't so careful. In fact, one of them said to you, "Hey! Cheat a little! At least you'll get the full double turn!"

That was puzzling, until you suddenly realized what he was suggesting. The next time you tried the double *tour*, you almost turned too far! But at least you could control it now. What was the secret shared by your friend?

LEAPS IN THE AIR are an impressive aspect of any form of dance, but leaps or jumps with simultaneous rotations involve an additional dimension. The turns to be described here are rotations around a vertical or inclined axis, from a half-turn to two full turns while in the air, from a running start or from a *plié* at rest. The first challenge to the dancer is to use the interaction between the foot (or feet) and the floor to generate not only the vertical force that produces the jump, but also the horizontal forces that produce the torque to initiate the turn. The second challenge is to control the rotation in the air after leaving the floor; the third is to get rid of the downward speed and the turning motion upon landing. One of the movements to be analyzed can create the illusion of initiating the turn after leaving the floor, in clear violation of a law of nature. In another, there is the illusion of a pause in the turning motion near the peak of the jump.

Rotational momentum is again the important quantity, since it must be constant during the time the body is in the air when no forces or torques can act on it.

The Demi-fouetté

The *demi-fouetté* is a jump with a half-turn after a running (or stepping) start. If takeoff is from the right foot, then the left leg kicks to the front as the right foot pushes off from the floor. The left leg remains oriented toward the direction of motion while the rest of the body flips through its 180° rotation to the right, landing back on the right leg, facing the direction from which the dancer came. In figure 5.2, Benjamin Pierce is shown in the three main stages of the *demi-fouetté* on the floor; the movement is also often performed with a vertical jump. Note that very little torque needs to be exerted against the floor, because the gesture leg, in which most of the rotational inertia resides, maintains its direction in space. Only the torso, head, supporting leg, and arms must revolve around the axis of rotation during the turn in the air, and those parts of the body are close to the rotation axis.

In fact, suppose this movement is carried out with *no* torque against the floor. In this case the total rotational momentum of the body remains zero, still allowing part of the body to rotate in one direction while another part rotates in the opposite

FIGURE 5.1. Adam Lüders performing a *grand jeté en tournant* in the New York City Ballet production of *Bournonville Divertissements*. Martha Swope/TimePix.

direction. The torso, head, and arms can rotate a full 180° to the right while the gesture leg revolves to the left. The movement of the extended gesture leg is small, since it is far from the axis of rotation and its rotational inertia is large. An approximation to a good *demi-fouetté* can be carried out in this way. (This technique of turning with zero rotational momentum is a part of the complicated movements a cat executes when righting itself in the air after being dropped upside down.)

In fact, most dancers do acquire some rotational momentum so that the gesture leg remains in its original direction while the rest of the body rotates through its 180° turn.

FIGURE 5.2.
Benjamin Pierce performing
a *demi-fouetté* on the floor.
This movement is often done
with a jump into the air
during the rotation.

The Tour Jeté *(Grand Jeté en Tournant)*

The *tour jeté,* or *grand jeté en tournant,* is also a jump with a 180° turn around a vertical axis. But in this movement the dancer lands on the foot *opposite* to the takeoff foot. The dancer faces the direction of motion when he takes off from his right foot and kicks a straight left leg into the air in front of him. After takeoff, his right leg moves up to meet the left, and he does a half-turn to the right, landing on the left leg, right leg to the rear, and facing in the direction from which he came. The sequence of photographs in figure 5.3 shows Sean Lavery in consecutive stages of the *tour jeté* described.

Ballet dancers being taught this movement often hear an instruction something like "Square your shoulders and hips! The turn is most brilliant when you rise straight up and then start to turn right at the peak of the jump!" When laws of physics are applied to such a model of the movement, one quickly concludes that such a feat would involve a violation of conservation of rotational momentum. (See appendix B.) But when this movement is performed by an accomplished dancer, one does indeed see the body apparently turning in the air *after* contact with the ground has ended. How is this illusion created, and how can a dancer maximize the effectiveness of the illusion? Rhonda Ryman has provided some insights into this movement.[1] The analysis is complex and best carried out mathematically, but a qualitative description is presented here.

If the body is undergoing a net rotation while in the air, there clearly must be some rotational momentum associated with this turn. But there can be no rotational momentum unless there has been some torque acting on the body. Once the body has lost contact with the floor, there is no longer a source of torque, so whatever rotational momentum existed at the moment of takeoff is maintained throughout the flight phase of the movement. The torque must be exerted against the floor before takeoff, so that the turning motion is established. But when the foot leaves the floor,

1. Rhonda Ryman, "Classical Ballet Technique: Separating Fact from Fiction," *York Dance Review* 5 (1976): 16. See also Rhonda Ryman, "A Kinematic and Descriptive Analysis of Selected Classical Ballet Skills" (master of arts thesis, York University, Toronto, Ont., 1976).

FIGURE 5.3. Sean Lavery performing a *tour jeté*. Note that the rotation has begun while the legs are approaching each other and stops when the rotational inertia is large in the final *arabesque* position aloft.

the body has a large rotational inertia (see appendix B) because the body's mass is distributed far from the axis of rotation. The left leg is extended to the front, the right foot has just left the floor to the rear, and the arms are in front of the body moving up. Since the rotational momentum is equal to the product of the rotational inertia and the turning rate, that turning rate can be quite small when the body mass is spread far from the axis of rotation. But there is *some* rotation, as seen in the second view of Sean's *tour jeté* in figure 5.3, in which his body has turned somewhat as he approaches the peak of the jump.

At the peak of the jump, the legs cross close to each other along the axis of rotation, and the arms simultaneously come together overhead, also close to the axis. Thus the rotational inertia is decreased substantially at that time, and the rate of rotation increases accordingly. The appearance to an observer is that the body has suddenly acquired its rotation at the peak of the jump. Upon descent, the arms open to the side and the right leg extends to the rear in *arabesque*, thus increasing the rotational inertia again and slowing the turn rate.

This analysis provides some clues to the dancer as to how to maximize the illusion of turning sharply at the peak of the jump. The legs must cross close to each other and the arms must come overhead *at the time the jump has reached its peak* in order to accomplish the decrease in rotational inertia at that moment, with the associated increase in turn rate. The body must approach a straight-line configuration as closely as possible so that the mass is close to the longitudinal rotation axis. Note from the photograph of the *tour jeté* (figure 5.3) that the axis is inclined somewhat from the vertical at the peak of the jump when the rotation is occurring.

It is important to note that these characteristics of the well-executed *tour jeté* that are necessary for the illusion of "flipping" around at the peak of the jump are consistent with the aesthetic goal of a successful *tour jeté* according to classical ballet standards. But the reasons for those characteristics are now seen to be not only aesthetic or stylistic but also based on compatibility with physical principles that *must* apply to the movement.

Another style of *tour jeté* emphasizes an aspect of the movement different from the illusion of flipping over in the air described above. It also applies a different physical principle. In this case the gesture leg kicks to the front, and the rest of the body turns *while* that leg is far from the axis of rotation and therefore has a large rotational inertia. That is, the first part of this movement is identical to the *demi-fouetté* described earlier. But after the torso, head, and arms have rotated through 180°, the legs are reversed through a scissors motion so that the landing is again to the foot opposite to the takeoff foot. In this form of the *tour jeté* the body flips to an *arabesque* position in the air very early, and then the legs reverse position. The impression is that the upper body floats down gracefully after the quick turning motion is completed. Whereas the first type of *tour jeté* depends upon a change in the body's shape, allowing a rapid rotation of the whole body near the peak of the jump, the latter type involves allowing all the body except the free leg to rotate in one direction while the free leg remains far from the rotation axis, and then reversing the legs late in the movement.

The Saut de Basque

Let us look now at the *saut de basque*, another jumping turn. (Hannah Wiley has carried out a comprehensive study of the *saut de basque*.)[2] The right foot is again the push-off foot, and the left leg kicks forward in the direction of motion. In this movement, however, the body initially executes a quarter-turn so that the left leg, still extended in the direction of motion, is now extended to the side of the body in second position. (The arms are also extended to the sides at that time.) As the dancer approaches a landing on the left foot, his body rotates to the right to a position facing the audience, with the right leg in a *coupé* position (in front of the ankle of the left leg). This movement is illustrated in the sequence of photographs of Sean in figure 5.4.

The jump in this movement involves the same principles discussed in chapter 3. The height of the jump is enhanced by the transfer of horizontal linear momentum to the vertical direction. That transfer must be controlled so that the linear motion is stopped at the end of the movement, or some motion is retained if the following

2. Hannah Wiley, "Laws of Motion Controlling Dance Movement: A Qualitative and Kinematic Analysis of *Saut de Basque*" (master's thesis, New York University, 1981).

FIGURE 5.4. Sean Lavery performing a *saut de basque* jumping turn. Note that the body turns little until the right leg comes in to the *retiré* position, which decreases the total rotational inertia.

movement continues traveling. The height of the jump must, of course, be sufficient to accomplish the turning motion while in the air, although the landing must be made slightly *before* the body faces the audience so that the supporting foot can exert the torque against the floor for a time long enough to decrease the rotational momentum back to zero.

As we have seen before, once the body leaves the floor, there is no more torque, and the rotational momentum must be a constant until landing. The torque must be exerted by the takeoff foot before it leaves the floor. (There is no possibility of a torque from *both* feet, since the two feet are not in contact with the floor at the same time in the running steps preceding the jump.) Note the importance of the full foot being in contact with the floor at the beginning of the jump so that the torque can be as large as possible. When the heel leaves the floor, very little torque can be exerted by the small area of the foot remaining in contact.

When the legs and arms are extended, the rotational inertia is large, and the body seems to pause in its rotation, a characteristic of a well-executed *saut de basque*. As the left leg approaches vertical in preparation for the landing, and the arms and right leg are brought in closer to the rotation axis, the rotational inertia decreases significantly, and the body turns rapidly. The landing, with the retarding torque exerted by the supporting foot, completes the *saut de basque* turn. Again, it is important to lower the left heel to the floor so that the full length of the foot is involved in the retarding torque.

Note that *too much* momentum would make it difficult to stop the turn at the end, since at that time there is only one foot on the floor that can exert the retarding torque against the floor. And the timing of the pause with arms and leg extended is crucially important. If they remain extended for too long a time, the faster rotation that occurs after they are retracted will not occur before the landing. If the arms and leg are brought in too soon, there will be too much rotation with the smaller rotational inertia, and the movement will not end facing the audience.

The double *saut de basque* is usually performed without the pause with extended arms and left leg. The reason is clear. In order to accomplish two full turns (actually one and three-quarters), the rotational inertia must be kept as small as

FIGURE 5.5.
A double *saut de basque* turn, in which the rotational inertia must be kept small throughout the movement in order for the necessary rate of turn to be maintained. The position shown here, rather than the extended position seen in figure 5.4, is maintained through most of the double turn.

possible so that the rotation rate is sufficiently large to accomplish the turn during the time in the air. The right leg may be in a *retiré* or *coupé* position during the turn, so that when the left leg is in *plié* after landing, the right leg does not drop to the floor. Figure 5.5 shows Sean near the peak of a double *saut de basque*, in which his body is much closer to the axis of rotation as he rotates than is the case with the "spread" position near the peak of the single turn.

The Turning Assemblé

The turning *assemblé* is similar to the *saut de basque* except the legs are straight and close to vertical, and the landing is made to both feet. The arms are usually overhead during the turn. In this case the rotational inertia is quite small, since the body mass is as close to the axis of rotation as possible. The turn can be quite rapid, and double turns are easier than the double *saut de basque*.

One aspect of the turning *assemblé* is worth noting. If the rotational inertia is small at the *beginning* of the movement, while the takeoff foot is exerting the torque against the floor, it will be difficult to acquire sufficient rotational momentum. The body will rotate away from its initial orientation too rapidly to allow the torque to have its effect in producing the rotational momentum needed. It will be difficult to accomplish the double turn during the time in the air, because the turn rate cannot be significantly increased after takeoff. If the rotational inertia is larger at the beginning, then it can be decreased after takeoff, thereby speeding the turn.

Although the left leg may extend somewhat during the initial phase, the arms are most important. The arms should extend and begin rotating in the direction of the turn before contact with the floor is lost, thereby absorbing much of the rotational momentum generated by the torque from the foot before the body rotates very far. The arms then move to the overhead position, and the rotational momentum resides in the whole body as it turns. The arms moving directly from side to overhead, rather than moving down in front and then overhead, reinforces the quick decrease in rotational inertia, making the turn more effective.

If the landing is in fifth position, the feet are close together, and exerting torque to *stop* the turn is difficult. It is again necessary to land before the turn is completed, allowing the body to slow to a stop in the desired direction.

The Tour en l'Air

The double *tour en l'air*, unlike the turns in the air described up to this point, usually starts from rest. For preparation, the feet are normally planted in fifth position (feet touching each other, toe to heel and heel to toe), the *plié* is fairly deep, and the arms are rotated a bit for a "windup." The turn is then performed with the body compacted as close to the vertical axis of rotation as possible in order to maximize the rotational velocity while the body is in the air. The legs are straight, together, and vertical, and the arms are close in front of the body. The head spots twice during the double turn.

This is the situation described at the beginning of the chapter, in which you could not get around the full two turns. Evidently you were generating too little torque. Ah! That's why you were advised to "cheat" a bit. Although to be "correct" the feet should be in a tight fifth position in preparation for a *tour en l'air*, most dancers find that the torque against the floor is too small (because of the small distance between the lines along which the equal and opposite forces act), and separating the feet somewhat makes the turn easier. In fact, separating the feet by only 3 inches or so, probably undetectable by all but the most perceptive observers, allows the distance between the forces to double, allowing for double the torque!

Suppose the horizontal forces from the two feet are not equal. Then those unequal forces will not be balanced and will produce a horizontal acceleration of the body's center of gravity. The motion will not be totally vertical. A common error is to distort the body somewhat (buttocks pushed back, for instance) in the *plié* immediately preceding the jump. The effect is to put more weight on one foot, tending to make that foot push harder horizontally, thus throwing the body off balance in the jump.

Either of two aspects of the *tour en l'air* may be emphasized when performing this movement. The horizontal forces exerted by the feet against the floor produce the torque that results in the rotational momentum for the turn. The vertical force exerted by the feet pushing down against the floor produces the height of the jump that allows the body time to rotate. Emphasizing the horizontal forces will produce a rapid turn without much height; pushing harder vertically and sacrificing horizontal force will produce greater height but a slower turn, with more time in the air in which to complete two full revolutions. The choice is a matter of style.

Any movement that ends in a static position must involve some forces or torques that remove the momentum associated with the movement. When the *tour en l'air* is completed to a static position, the feet must have sufficient friction with the floor to exert the retarding torque necessary. Thus again the body must return to the floor *slightly* before completion of the turn so that it may coast to a stop facing the audience. If the rotational inertia is increased (by extending the arms, for instance) as the body coasts to a stop, the rotation rate decreases so that there is little turning after landing. The decreased turn rate at the end makes the direction the body is facing when landing less critical than if the body were continuing its rapid rotation.

A Final Leap

All of the turns analyzed in this chapter have involved torques, rotation speeds, and rotational momenta previously described for *pirouettes*. The jump has added some complications because of the combination of two kinds of motion. But the power of the physical analyses is particularly evident as these more complicated and impressive movements succumb to careful scrutiny.

One form of effective *tour jeté* involves an illusion that requires controlling the rotation rate while in the air. The legs and arms must briefly be brought as close as possible to the straight line around which the body is rotating at the time the peak of the jump is reached. This allows the rotation rate to increase substantially at that time, creating the illusion of flipping around at the peak of the movement. The *demi-fouetté*, similar to the *tour jeté*, requires less (even zero) rotational momentum, and hence less torque, because the gesture leg maintains its orientation in space rather than revolving. A second type of *tour jeté* is effectively a *demi-fouetté* followed by a reversal of the legs so that the landing is to the foot opposite to the takeoff foot.

The *saut de basque* involves a similar control of the turn rate in the air, but this time the body is *extended* at the peak of the jump so as to create the illusion of *pausing* briefly in the turn. Since the takeoff and landing both involve just one foot, the accelerating and slowing torques require the full foot to be on the floor, maximizing the effectiveness of the foot in exerting the required torques. The double *saut de basque* turn eliminates the "pause," because the body must remain compact in order to maintain the turn rate required for two full turns before landing.

The turning *assemblé* and the *tour en l'air* both require careful control of the rotational inertia of the body. It must be as large as feasible before takeoff so that the turn is relatively slow while torque is being exerted against the floor. After takeoff, the rotational inertia is decreased to provide a rapid turn rate. The arms, in addition to contributing to a large rotational inertia when they are extended at the beginning of the movement, also absorb some of the initial rotational momentum by rotating relative to the body at the beginning of the turn. When in the air, the whole body shares the total rotational momentum. In both of these turns, the landing must be made slightly before the turn is completed so that the body can coast to its final orientation while slowing to a stop. The elimination of momentum can result only from the retarding torque exerted by the feet against the floor.

A low, rapid *tour en l'air* is created by emphasizing the horizontal force couple exerted by the feet against the floor, while a high jump with a slower turn results from emphasizing the vertical force. The proper emphasis will, of course, depend on the tempo of the music and the character of the choreography.

One important way to control the timing of the body rotation is to control how the arms move. Their rotation can be isolated from that of the rest of the body, and if they are far from the axis of rotation, they can carry a substantial rotational momentum. Thus coordination of the arms is an important aspect of both the style and the mechanics of the turns discussed in this chapter.

Turns in other styles of dance than classical ballet will also involve the control of the important mechanical parameters of the movement: rotational speed, body position and configuration, and the appropriate accelerating and decelerating torques against the floor. The physical analyses in this chapter can be applied to any turns for which the characteristics are sufficiently specifiable and understood.

When any of these rotations with jumps are observed, two movements are happening at once. Dancers are challenged to coordinate the two movements so that, for instance, a landing does indeed occur as the desired amount of total rotation has been accomplished. Unlike linear velocity, which can be changed only by means of forces from outside the body, rotational velocity can be changed by controlling the body's distribution of mass relative to the rotation axis, even when in the air where there is no contact with a source of force. This fact provides an additional degree of freedom for dancers, but also makes the control physically more complex. This combination of freedom and necessary control contributes to the visual effect of these rotations in the air.

6　*The* PAS DE DEUX

"Haven't you ever heard of rosin?" your partner growled. Once more your feet had slipped on the floor and caused a most ungraceful fall from that beautiful arched pose, leaning way back with your arms overhead almost touching the floor, your partner's arm supporting you around your back.

"I told you, we aren't allowed to use rosin on this floor. And look! Others are making it work!"

When you thought about the pose, and the force making your feet slip, you suddenly realized where that unwanted force came from and what your partner could do to solve the problem! So you spoke to him just as the director was stomping over to see why you couldn't make this simple pose work. And when you tried it once more, it worked perfectly!

What idea had you shared with your partner?

INTERACTIONS BETWEEN performing artists vary. The dramatic arts almost always involve performers interacting with each other. In music, orchestra members must, of course, interact with a conductor and with each other. Musical interaction is particularly profound in jazz, where the sensitivity of each musician to the improvised music being created by others is the primary challenge and source of appeal for both the performer and the listener. But interaction between performers is perhaps strongest in dance, in which the medium of the art form is the human body itself.

Why do so many people find partnered dance particularly appealing? On one level we can see a dancer interacting with another in a way that must involve two minds sharing interpretation and artistic sensibilities while their bodies are responding to the physical forces resulting from the interaction. The images can be gender neutral, with interactions that are symmetric between men and women, or as is usually the case in classical ballet, the images can involve interactions that are distinctly different in the roles, purposes, and styles of men and women. In any form, partnering in dance creates a compelling image because of the basic human need to interact, both mentally and physically, with other people. The *pas de deux* in dance represents such an interaction that can elicit a strong response from observers.

The History and Appeal of the Pas de Deux

In the early days of formalized Western dance, partnering arose out of social dancing, not designed to be observed by audiences. "The steps . . . differed little from those of the era's ballroom dances; the theatrical form was simply more polished and studied."[1] Men and women began to dance together for the entertainment of others in the late seventeenth century, but at that time female roles were often played by men or boys.

The *pas de deux* as an important aspect of dance gained major impetus in the romantic era of ballet beginning with Marie Taglioni in the 1830s. As romantic

1. Jack Anderson, *Ballet and Modern Dance: A Concise History* (Princeton Book Co., 1986), p. 25.

FIGURE 6.1. Merrill Ashley and Ib Andersen in the New York City Ballet production of Balanchine's *Ballade*. Martha Swope/TimePix.

ballets evolved during the nineteenth century, partners acted out romantic stories involving young princesses and their cavaliers. There were definite gender roles in which the woman was delicate and dependent, the man strong, supportive, and controlling. The role of the man in helping to display his partner in the most effective way was established, as was the general format of these ballets. In fact, the primary role of the male dancer in ballet became, in the late nineteenth century, one of

FIGURE 6.2. Julie Kent and Benjamin Pierce in a pose in which he supports her in a position she would find it difficult to maintain without him.

support for his partner. It took Nijinsky, near the turn of the century, to bring the role of men back to full dancing participation.

There are general differences in partnering technique in different styles of dance that are quite apparent to the perceptive observer. For instance, in ballroom dance one can notice that the transitions are smoother than in ballet. That is, when a supported *pirouette* is performed in the ballet style, there is a clear preparation moment when the woman establishes her position, with her partner behind her, and then they start the turn. In ballroom dance one is more likely to see a smooth transition in which the turn springs seamlessly out of some previous movement. And at the end of the ballet turn, the ballerina usually takes a pose and stops, then moves into the next movement, whereas the ballroom dancers will meld the end of the turn smoothly into the next steps. Reasons for these and other differences can be sought and may involve, for instance, the fact that the precarious nature of dancing *en pointe* requires a more careful preparation for movements. Of course, any generalizations have their exceptions, but a sensitive observer can be intrigued not only by these "normal" stylistic differences but by the occasional exceptions as well.

As dancers became more proficient and comfortable in the roles they were expected to fill, and men in particular brought more athleticism to dance, the level of difficulty of partnered movements increased. The Russians introduced aspects of movement from the circus environment, giving rise to the big lifts that are often seen in the *pas de deux* of today and the twentieth century. It was discovered that if personal danger was involved in the more athletic moves carried out by partners, audience appeal was heightened. A woman carried aloft at arm's length above her partner can create several vicarious images for the observer: the exhilaration of flying; the need for trust in another person's strength and goodwill; acceptance of the dangerous possibility of falling from that height; and of course the demonstration of rare skill in a demanding art form.

Traditionally, the roles of men and women have been quite distinct; only recently have the expectations of these distinctions been suppressed. But the traditional roles were built around the known average anatomical differences between men and women. The average man is taller, heavier, and stronger than the average woman. The woman, however, is more likely to have greater flexibility, allowing a greater range of line represented by body position. So if one partner is to provide lifting or other forces on the body of the other, it is traditionally the man supporting the woman. If support allows a partner to display pleasing body line more effectively, it is the woman who is traditionally provided with that support.

One can speculate on other reasons for the way gender differentiation in the *pas de deux* evolved. It is the male who must be more sensitive to the interpretation of the dance by his partner, responding to the subtleties of the woman's timing and style. Sensitivity and communication are characteristics usually attributed to women more than men. It is intriguing to note that jazz is a performing art in which women are dramatically underrepresented, although it is particularly demanding of artistic sensitivity to other people. Perhaps both jazz and partnered dance attract men who crave an outlet for their artistic sensitivity to a performing partner.

It is now true that traditional differentiations between male and female roles in society are changing. Dance, as a reflection of society, incorporates those changes. *Pas de deux* movements are now seen in all combinations rather than just the traditional role-differentiated male/female combination, and the constraints of the traditional gender differentiations are often removed. But the average anatomical differences between men and women remain. The partnering movements seen in traditional classical ballet are compatible with those average differences, in that the man uses his strength to provide support and the woman uses her shape and flexibility to show a graceful line. When partnered dance removes the constraints of that traditional style, the movements are likely to be quite different, not involving the same sorts of lifts and supported *pirouettes*. On the other hand, there are interactive movements that two strong men can carry out that might be difficult for a man and a woman. And our society is increasingly open to noncompetitive physical interaction between men.

Another basis for the appeal of partnered dance is the vicarious pleasure one gains from seeing an activity one cannot imagine participating in personally. Most people do not have access to a partner who can carry out the sorts of interactions displayed in a *pas de deux*. The coordination necessary to do the more impressive moves seen in partnering—supported *pirouettes* and big lifts, for instance—is only possible for those who have the appropriate strength, body, and training. There is the fantasy of imagining oneself participating in those movements. There is also the fantasy component of idealized romantic love in the *pas de deux* of classical ballet. The guilt sometimes associated with enjoyment of erotica is removed; the observed interactions between dancers involve physical contact and the appearance of romance without the overtly sexual images that our society has defined as erotic. Watching a *pas de deux* can be a "clean" way to enjoy sexual images.

For a variety of reasons, two dancers working together and interacting with each other can inspire in the observer a unique response unlike the response to solo dancers. The aim of the dancers is to project an aesthetic image to the audience that

FIGURE 6.3. Cynthia Harvey and Guillaume Graffin in *Manon* for American Ballet Theatre.

represents a "conversation" between the two partners. As Cynthia Harvey, retired principal dancer at American Ballet Theatre, has said, "When experiencing the *pas de deux* in performance, I often come away hoping that the audience was captivated by our 'conversation' as much as by the excitement of the physicality. It is so satisfying when the *pas de deux* goes well."[2]

The appeal of the *pas de deux* is enhanced when there is clear mutual respect between the dancers and an obvious joy expressed in their dancing. As Cynthia has commented, "Sometimes when the *pas de deux* is seamless, I am gratified beyond belief. No solo has ever provided me with the satisfaction I have derived from a well-danced, sensitively portrayed *pas de deux*. Poetically speaking, when it comes to communicating life's great range of emotions, a *pas de deux* can ultimately be the

2. Kenneth Laws, and Cynthia Harvey, *Physics, Dance, and the Pas de Deux* (Schirmer Books, 1994), p. 99.

finest balletic merging that there is. And finally, the *pas de deux* is one of the most pleasurable experiences of the dance."[3]

Who's Responsible for What?

One of the greatest challenges in successful partnering is to figure out the division of responsibilities. In solo work, the dancer has only one body and mind to deal with. One of the dancer's constraints is, of course, the limit of technical capability. Other constraints are imposed by the environment: the tempo of the music determined by a conductor or instrumentalist, the vagaries of the stage or studio floor and the shoes in contact with that floor, the size of the space available, and the variables of weather, lights, and mental state. The solo dancer copes alone with a physical environment that is, if not always controllable, at least mostly predictable. The floor does not suddenly change its position, and gravity does not suddenly release its hold on us!

A dancer working with a partner must consider the somewhat unpredictable interaction with another person who also has the same individual concerns. Much effort in rehearsal is invested in trying to learn to predict how a partner will move—how the partner will interpret the music and how the physical interaction between the two people is to be accomplished.

But now, with two people controlling the movement, opportunities for conflict arise. Men are well aware of the difficulty caused by a partner who tries to maintain her own balance by those techniques discussed in chapter 2. And women are aware of the problems caused by men who fail to stop a supported *pirouette* at the right place so that she can end the movement *en pointe*. A physical analysis of the forces involved can help lead to resolution of uncertainties.

Analyses of those forces and torques involved in partnered dance are the subject of most of this and the next two chapters. But what are the underlying reasons for the responsibilities borne by each partner?

3. Laws and Harvey, *Physics, Dance, and the Pas de Deux*, p. 101.

FIGURE 6.4. Julie Kent and Benjamin Pierce in a "swan" pose. Who is responsible for the forces that keep her from falling or from collapsing in the upper body? This is an example of the shared responsibility in partnered dance.

The woman bears the responsibility for much of the style and imagery of the dance. It is very important for her to feel free and to have the ability to move in her partner's arms and hands with trust rather than tension and struggle. She needs to rely on his strength and stability. The effort shouldn't show as the ballerina performs moves that would be precarious or even impossible alone. The sense of freedom in turn creates the confidence that allows a ballerina to execute difficult and exciting moves.

One challenge to the male partner is to judge just how much guidance and help his partner needs so that he can provide the necessary support while giving her a feeling of freedom and confidence. That depends on how secure the woman is with each particular movement (assuming unforeseen occurrences are avoided). That is, the woman may prefer to do a *pirouette* totally on her own, only depending on her partner to hold her on balance at the end. Or she may prefer to have some turning force from her partner at the beginning to give her additional rotational momentum, and may prefer to have him guiding her waist throughout the turn in order to keep her on balance. *Pirouettes* may require little support from the partner unless something unforeseen happens. If the *pirouette* is unexpectedly off balance at the beginning, the male partner must, through forces he exerts on her waist, adjust her position to bring her back to balance by the end of the turn.

Some movements require a much stronger participation from the supporting partner than others. For an overhead lift, the woman can do little to control the way she is held aloft, although she is primarily responsible for the position she maintains while in the air.

Physical Interactions between Partners

What sorts of physical interactions are important in partnered dance? We know that forces produce movement, but we need to agree on what we mean by "movement." A person can move individual body parts—arms, legs, head—without any external forces acting on the body as a whole. The forces can originate from within the body. But a change in state of motion of the body as a whole—movement across the floor, a vertical motion, or a rotation—requires a force acting on the body from outside the body.

The source of such forces that move the body as a whole can only be the floor, gravity, or a partner. A partner can exert a horizontal force that will change the state of a dancer's linear movement across the floor; a vertical force may produce a lift; "push-pull" forces may produce rotations. If a partner pushes on a dancer at the center of gravity of her body, there is *only* a linear acceleration or deceleration, and no rotational motion. But a force on the body not at the center of gravity will generally induce a rotation, wanted or unwanted, in addition to a linear movement.

Carrying out those interactions smoothly requires coordination. One example is a vertical lift. If a man lifting his partner waits for her to jump before he lifts, he is too late. But if the woman waits for him to lift before she jumps, he will be lifting dead weight. In either case, the smoothness of the movement is lost and the lifter is vulnerable to injury. If the two partners are coordinated, the lifting force varies more smoothly, allowing for greater height in the lift and more grace in the movement.

Another example of the need for coordination is a supported *pirouette* (described in more detail in the next chapter). For any *pirouette*, the forces initiating the turn may be a result of the woman's forces against the floor or of forces exerted on her by her partner or both; balance also may be controlled by either the woman or her partner. In any case, two minds must be "in synch," using visual cues, the music, and experience with the particular partner. Clearly, the timing and unity of interpretation cannot be perfect between two different human minds, but the audience is offered the opportunity of seeing how close the two minds can come to a perfect union. That is part of the magic of the *pas de deux*.

Balance

Early in a typical *pas de deux*, one often sees slow gestures and poses, often requiring careful balance, which gradually lead to more active movements later in the dance. These poses establish the image the dance is supposed to convey. The subtle tilts of the heads, gestures with the arms, and looks in the eyes give the audience clues about what to expect in the way of interaction between these two people.

Support from a partner can allow for a wider variety of static positions for these gestures and poses than is possible for a dancer alone. A static position of a solo dancer implies balance, which requires the dancer's center of gravity to lie on a vertical line through the area of support at the floor. But other positions, not necessarily obeying that requirement, are possible when forces from a partner can help produce the condition of equilibrium. An example is a lunge, as described in the anecdote at the beginning of this chapter, in which the center of gravity of a woman may be displaced horizontally far from her feet, but the displaced weight is supported by forces exerted by the partner at her waist, torso, or other area of her

FIGURE 6.5. Benjamin Pierce holding Julie Kent in an off-balance position.

body. Sometimes an image of tension or impending movement can be created by a dancer in an off-balance position held by the partner.

Balance for a person alone, for whom the floor and gravity are the only sources of influence on her movement, was discussed in chapter 2. To maintain balance, subtle movements are necessary that result in the appropriate horizontal forces being exerted against the floor that keep the center of gravity directly above the supporting foot. Now suppose that the dancer has a partner and does not have to carry out those subtle movements to maintain her own balance. The partner can exert the appropriate horizontal forces on her that she needs, often at her waist but also sometimes through contact at the hand or other places on the body. Note that some of the most impressive moments in a *pas de deux* occur when a woman, having established balance with the help of her partner, is suddenly released from his support and balances on her own. (A familiar example occurs in the third act of *Sleeping*

Beauty during the famous Rose Adagio.) Achieving that necessary balanced condition with a partner prior to the release is a difficult feat, requiring sensitive control from the partner and timing of the release by the woman.

Maintaining a ballerina's balance when she is working with a partner is a challenge. She is used to dancing alone and depending on her own movements to maintain her own balance. If she tries to do that when a partner is also trying to control her balance, she creates a problem quite common in dancers learning *pas de deux*. He cannot know where her body is if she is carrying out those subtle adjusting movements while his hands are trying to be in the right place to support her. Teamwork is required in this most fundamental of interactions.

Consider now a case in which the woman must change her position while maintaining balance. Suppose she is holding an *arabesque* position facing stage left, standing on her left supporting leg with her right leg extended behind her. Her partner's hands are at her waist. Now she moves into a *penché*, as shown in figure 6.6, pivoting forward on her supporting leg, upper body bending forward and down, and working leg rising toward the vertical. If she is *en pointe*, it is her partner's job to maintain her balance while she carries out this movement. Since her center of gravity shifts due to the forward and backward movement of her upper body and working leg, her partner must shift the location of her waist appropriately in order to maintain her balance. Most women find it easier to stay *en pointe* if they are held in a position slightly forward of true balance, because the forward weight of the body helps to keep the toes under the supporting foot, as demonstrated in figure 6.6. That effect is strongest in women without much arch in the foot. A good partner will be sensitive to such subtle differences in the dancers with whom he works. And there is more to the partner's job in this simple movement than has just been described. He provides some lift and torque at her waist to help her rise to recover from the *penché* position.

A partner's two hands at the woman's waist provide the strongest support for her movements. But sometimes contact is more tenuous. An example of a balance with contact only at the hands occurs in the Rose Adagio section of *Sleeping Beauty*. In this section Aurora, the title character, dances with a group of four suitors vying

FIGURE 6.6.
An *arabesque penché*,
also off balance for
Julie Kent.

for her hand in marriage. She dances with each of them in turn, and one of the more challenging sections involves long balances of Aurora in *attitude* (similar to *arabesque* but with a bent back leg), supported by one hand in the hand of each of the suitors in turn, balancing alone in the transitions between partners. She faces stage right, in sequence facing each suitor in *attitude* on her right supporting leg with her left leg behind her, her right hand in contact with his right hand. The sequence is later repeated, this time with a full promenade in a circle with each partner in turn, as demonstrated by Julie Kent and Benjamin Pierce in figure 6.7. The dancer must remain facing her partner while balanced *en pointe* throughout each of these long maneuvers, a most impressive feat!

If Aurora is balanced with contact at the hand of a partner, everything is fine. But, as before, she is eventually likely to find herself slightly off balance, particularly

during the promenades in the second sequence. How does she adjust for this loss of balance? If she pushes sideways against her partner's hand, she can indeed regain balance because of the horizontal force that his hand exerts on her in response. But such a horizontal force exerted on her body some distance from the vertical axis of potential rotation around her supporting foot will result in an undesired rotation of her body away from an orientation facing him. That is, suppose she starts falling toward her left. If she pushes toward the left against his hand, the response of his hand is to push toward her right, which not only moves her center of gravity back toward her right, helping her to regain balance, but also starts a rotation of her body to the right away from its orientation facing him.

How, then, does she maintain her balance? She must exert against his hand, not a linear force, but a *twisting torque*. That is, in the case described above, her hand must exert a clockwise twist against his hand to create the response that corrects balance without resulting in the unwanted rotation. An overhead view of the hand

FIGURE 6.7. Julie Kent and Benjamin Pierce in a promenade in *attitude*, in which she is responsible for maintaining her balance by the way she twists her hand against his hand while turning.

FIGURE 6.8.
In this overhead
view, Lisa de
Ribère and Sean
Lavery show the
proper position
of the hands for
maintaining bal-
ance during the
promenade of
figure 6.7.

positions is shown in figure 6.8. (A detailed description of this situation has been published previously.)[4]

Accelerating Motions

Another way a partner can make movements possible that would be impossible alone is by causing a dancer to accelerate horizontally. A solo dancer can do that only by exerting an appropriate horizontal force against the floor, which means that the movement must start with some toppling motion so that the feet don't run out from under the rest of the body. But with a partner, accelerations can take place from balanced positions, or even from positions that lean off balance away from the direction of acceleration. For example, consider a dancer in *arabesque* position on her right supporting leg facing stage right, with her left leg and hand behind her, and a partner behind her also. She leans forward (toward stage right), but her partner

4. Kenneth Laws, "Precarious Aurora—An Example of Physics in Partnering," *Kinesiology for Dance* 12 (August 1980).

pulls back on her left hand and accelerates her toward stage left. As she starts moving in that direction, she may execute a *fouetté* that rotates her to face the direction she starts moving. The effect is that of a tension pulling her in a direction opposite to her lean and is difficult to accomplish without a partner as a source of force.

Similarly, static positions that would be off balance for a solo dancer can be maintained by the forces provided by a partner. With less force from the partner, the leaning *arabesque* described above can be a static pose with a powerful effect of unresolved tension.

Suppose a dancer wishes to move in a circular path. If dancing alone, the floor is the only source of force directed toward the inside of the circle—a force necessary for such a curved path. The dancer must be leaning toward the inside of the circle in order to be able to exert that force between the feet and the floor, for the same reason that a road is bankedat the curves, or a bicyclist leans into a turn. But if a partner is present, that person can provide the necessary force directed toward the center of the circular path. For instance, both partners can be rotating around each other, as is often observed in "pivot turns" in ballroom dance or in some folk dance movements. Both partners can be in off-balance positions such that, without the other person, they would fly off away from the circular path. Again, the image is that of a body being held in a path or pose from which it would like to break away.

Final Poses

A common way of concluding a *pas de deux* is for the man to be supporting his partner in some climactic pose at the end of the musical phrase or section. These poses may involve lifts, discussed in chapter 8, or other supported poses such as a "fish" or "swan" position. In both of these, the woman's partner holds her off the floor in an arched front-side-down position facing the audience. In the "fish," her partner supports her weight with one hand on her thigh and the other under her lower ribs, as shown in figure 6.9. In the "swan," shown in figure 6.4, the woman's weight is supported on her partner's forward (bent) leg while she prevents her upper

FIGURE 6.9.
A "fish" position, some-
times seen as a final pose
in a *pas de deux*.

body from falling forward and down by clamping one of her legs behind his back. The demand on the woman's back muscles is great, and the position is not easy to achieve.

Other final poses may involve a lunge, or fall, in which the woman falls to an inclined position, supported by her partner's arm, as described in the anecdote at the beginning of this chapter. Although this position looks straightforward, there are potential pitfalls that are not obvious to an observer. If the woman tries to keep her upper body more vertical by bending up at the waist, then the part of her body that her partner is trying to support with his arm is closer to vertical, and a vertical supporting force becomes very difficult. On the other hand, if his arm is too high on her body, he may be forcing her into that bent position. In the situation at the beginning of the chapter, the problem is that the woman's feet keep slipping out from under her. Note that her partner can keep her in equilibrium in one of two ways: (1) He can exert a vertical force on her back, balancing the downward force of gravity at her center of gravity. His upward force plus that of the floor acting at her feet will total her weight, and she is in equilibrium. (2) But it is also possible to exert a purely horizontal force on her body and, assuming sufficient friction at the floor, keep her in equilibrium. That is approximately the technique one uses when "walking" a tall ladder up a wall. But then, if friction is not sufficient, he succeeds not only in supporting her but also in pushing her across the floor! Your comment to your partner in the opening anecdote was to support you with a vertical force only, avoiding pushing sideways toward your feet. (A more detailed analysis of this situation is provided in appendix K.)

To the Next Step

Neither constant movement nor entirely static positions are seen in dance. Both are necessary to create the aesthetic images desired. Static poses, when used as breathing moments in a dance that is mostly movement, help expand the range of images possible. There are subtleties in the ways dancers use forces between themselves and their environment in order to maintain these balanced positions for just the right length of time, sometimes using large forces between partners, sometimes only a light touch.

Dancers moving alone have the entire range of human movement available to them within the constraints of their own bodies and technical capabilities and the constraints imposed by the physical reality of the floor and gravity as the sole sources of external force. Dancers working with partners must deal with the uncertainties arising from the lack of total individual control. But they have the advantage of the

FIGURE 6.10. Suzanne Farrell and Peter Martins in a scene from New York City Ballet's *Allegro Brillante*.

increased range of movements made possible by interactions with another body and mind. Those interactions expand the range of possible motion through the medium of the forces between the two bodies.

Two major categories of partnered dance movement call for more concentrated attention: turns and lifts. Turns of many kinds are discussed in chapter 7; lifts, a most impressive aspect of partnering, in chapter 8.

7 *The mechanics of* PARTNERED TURNS

"We should be getting more than two turns out of this!" You and your partner are having trouble with your whip turns, in which you start *en pointe*, one foot at the knee of the supporting leg, your partner standing behind you holding you by your waist. You extend your leg front, and then he applies forces to your body that start you turning. But it seems that your turn stops almost as soon as it starts! He keeps saying, "Bring your leg in sooner!" and talks about how ice skaters turn more rapidly when they bring their arms and legs closer to the axis of rotation. Well, something isn't working. Then you recall what you learned about *fouetté* turns earlier and suddenly realize that you've been doing exactly the opposite of what you should do to make the movement work!

What should you do, and why?

TURNING DANCERS ARE an integral part of virtually every dance ever choreo-graphed. These rotations can involve *pirouettes*, turns around a vertical axis on one supporting leg; promenades, slow, controlled turns around a vertical axis; and even impressive turns in the air. As we have seen, many of these turns can be per-formed alone; we now consider those that require the interaction of partners.

A normal supported *pirouette* consists of a woman executing a turn with the help of a partner behind her, usually with his hands on her waist. The partner can help provide the torque to initiate the turn, can help maintain her balance during the turn, and can provide the reverse torque to stop the turn in the desired orienta-tion. We will now consider those three phases of the turn, and the responsibilities of each partner in the turning process.

Starting a Supported Pirouette

We have seen that a solo dancer has only the floor to use as a source of forces that will produce either linear movement of the whole body or rotational motion around some axis. In many cases, the floor is used for the horizontal forces required to initi-ate a turn with a partner, and the dancer needs no help from the partner for the turning action itself. But a partner *can* exert forces on her waist that contribute to her total rotation or supply the entire torque that produces the rotation.

Let us examine *pirouettes* that are performed with the woman starting *en pointe* and depending totally on her partner for the torque that gives her the rota-tional momentum for the turn. That seems simple—he just pulls back with one hand and pushes forward with the other. Those are the two equal and opposite forces, acting with some distance between the lines along which those forces act, that produce the torque that starts the turn. The problem is that she quickly starts rotating as soon as those forces start acting, and he is no longer able to continue ex-erting the necessary forces. The resulting turn is not very effective.

But recall the *fouetté* turns described in chapter 4. That sequence involved a transfer of rotational momentum back and forth between a leg rotating in a hori-zontal plane and the body as a whole. A similar mechanism can be used in starting a

partnered *pirouette*, allowing the partner to extend the length of time he can exert a torque. Again, she uses a horizontal extended leg, which has a large rotational inertia. As shown in the sequence in figure 7.2, the movement starts with the woman *en pointe* on her left supporting leg with her right leg extended a little to the left of front (*croisé*), and her partner's hands at her waist. He starts pulling back with his right hand and pushing forward with his left, while she causes her right leg to revolve from front to her right side. During that time her torso, head, and supporting leg don't rotate, so her partner continues to exert those forces with his

FIGURE 7.1.
Cynthia Harvey
and Guillaume
Graffin in *Manon*
for American
Ballet Theatre.

FIGURE 7.2.
A whip turn performed by
Julie Kent and Benjamin
Pierce. Notice that the rotating leg temporarily stores the
momentum while the partner
is still able to exert forces
that increase the total momentum generated.

hands. Then, after she has gained significant rotational momentum, she brings her leg in to a normal *pirouette* position with the foot at the knee of the supporting left leg. The rotational momentum stored in that moving right leg is quickly transferred to the body as a whole, and a rapid rotation results.

When you had trouble performing the whip turns described at the beginning of this chapter, you were trying to maximize your turn rate by bringing your leg close to the supporting leg quickly as soon as you started rotating. But you were actually turning too soon, preventing your partner from exerting the torque for a long enough time to generate the necessary rotational momentum for an effective turn. When you rotated the leg from front to side, storing the momentum there while he continued to exert forces on your body, your turn was more effective!

When performing that whip turn, or "supported *fouetté* turn," as it is sometimes called, seldom do the participants or observers realize what a marvelous coordinated mechanism is at work in achieving an impressive turn rate! It becomes clear why certain aspects of that movement are important if it is to be carried out effectively. For instance, if her rotating leg takes a shortcut into the knee rather than moving all the way to the side, her whole body starts absorbing the rotational momentum significantly sooner, and the resulting momentum cannot be as great. Also, if her partner is not prepared to exert the forces at the same time she starts moving her leg, then the leg rotating in one direction will cause the rest of her body to react by rotating in the opposite direction.

There is another form of supported *pirouette*, called a finger turn. (See figure 7.3.) The dancer again begins *en pointe* with the right leg extended to the front and a little to the left (*croisé*). Her right hand is over her head, loosely clasped around her partner's downward-pointing finger, which acts as an axle around which she can turn. The axle overhead and her *pointe* shoe on the floor establish the vertical rotation axis. To start the turn, she pushes backward with her left hand against his left hand extended to the side, again swinging her right leg from front to side to extend the length of time she is able to push off from his hand. The right leg then returns to the normal *pirouette* position. The mechanical principles involved in this turn are similar to those applied to the supported *fouetté* turn shown in figure 7.2.

FIGURE 7.3.
An experiment at Dickinson
College designed to simulate the
finger turn and to measure the
effectiveness of different techniques for pushing off of the
partner's hand. The results
showed that significantly more
rotational momentum was
gained when the leg was carried
properly from front to side. The
dancer is Abi Stafford, pre-New
York City Ballet but older than
shown in figures P.2 and 1.4.
Photo by Pierce Bounds.

Several aspects of this turn are important. First, the partner must be sufficiently
tall to hold his finger strongly above the woman's head while she is *en pointe*. (In
these days of tall female dancers, that requirement is not trivial!) Second, it is crucially important for the woman to have her body well aligned along that vertical rotation axis, with the hand held *directly* above the supporting foot rather than somewhat to the front, which is a more natural position. Since the hand determines the
rotation axis, a hand in front of the vertical line will cause her partner to have to
move his hand in a circle while exerting the proper forces, which not only is difficult
but prevents him from maintaining the turn rate with an accelerating torque.

Experiments on finger turns were performed in 1998 at Dickinson College in order to quantify the difference in effectiveness of the turn depending on the technique used. The results showed that the total rotational momentum acquired by the dancer when she rotated the leg from front to side at the beginning of the turn was 2.3 times greater than when the leg started and remained in the *pirouette* position. The results, along with a description of the experimental technique used, were published in a journal article.[1]

A finger turn may be maintained by the male partner's supporting hand alone by appropriate movements and forces. If the supporting finger is rotated in a small circle above the woman's head, her axis of rotation will precess (revolve) around the vertical line through the supporting foot. If the force exerted by the supporting hand leads the precession of the rotation axis by 90°, the torque maintaining the turn rate will be most effective. This mechanism, pictured in the diagram in figure 7.4, is similar to the action used when swinging a weight on a string in a circle around the head.

Balance during a Supported Pirouette

A dancer performing a smooth and pleasing supported *pirouette* should be as close to balanced as possible, particularly at the end of the turn. Why is it difficult to maintain balance in a supported *pirouette*? First, it is unlikely that any *pirouette* can be started with the center of gravity so precisely positioned that it is directly over the point of the supporting foot. Second, because a partner is there to help control balance, a supported *pirouette* often lasts longer than a *pirouette* performed alone, which allows more time for toppling off balance. Third, the body performing a *pirouette* is not in a symmetric configuration, so there is always some inherent wobble of body mass around the axis of rotation. This wobble can be exaggerated if the woman is also trying to avoid hitting her partner with a knee or elbow during the rotation. Finally, the turning dancer's partner cannot clamp his

1. Kenneth Laws, "Momentum Transfer in Dance Movement," *Medical Problems of Performing Artists* 13, no. 4 (December 1998): 136–45.

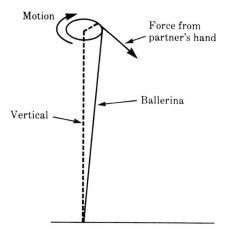

Motion

Force from
partner's hand

Vertical

Ballerina

FIGURE 7.4.
This diagram shows the direction of the force from the supporting partner's hand necessary to maintain the rotation in a finger turn. Note that the hand must move in a small circle, pulling the turning dancer around a vertical axis.

hand on any part of her body. Since she is rotating, she is constantly slipping through his hands.

First, let us suppose the ballerina is in a nonrotating *pirouette* position (supporting leg straight, *en pointe*, with the gesture leg raised to the side with its foot at the knee of the supporting leg). It is clear that if her center of gravity is displaced horizontally from the region directly above the small area of support at the floor, the partner merely has to exert a horizontal force at her waist in the appropriate direction to return her to a balanced position. If she meanwhile is trying to regain her own balance by the techniques described in chapter 2, she is making her partner's job difficult. And the partner's contribution to her balance *is* necessary if she is to maintain balance longer than she would if performing the movement alone. One of the hardest jobs for a woman learning to be partnered is to prevent herself from doing those balance-regaining body manipulations that are so important when she is dancing solo. She is far more often dancing alone than with a partner, so those subtle adjusting movements become habit. But those same movements prevent a partner from knowing where her body is and what he has to do to correct her imbalance.

Suppose now that she is rotating. Her job is to be as close to balance as possible at the beginning of the turn but to avoid trying to maintain her balance once she is turning. It is more difficult, however, for her partner to control her balance

THE MECHANICS OF PARTNERED TURNS

when she is rotating than when she is not. If her waist were frictionless, then forces between his hands and her waist could easily be directed such as to return her to balance. But there is a friction force also, in a direction tangent to the hand/waist contact. When she is balanced, that friction force will be the same from both hands. But if he is exerting a greater force with one hand than the other in order to move her back toward balance from a sideways displacement, the friction force from that hand will be greater also, and she will have a tendency to move forward or backward.

That is, suppose the woman is starting to topple to the right, while turning to her right. Her partner uses his right hand to push her back toward the left. But if he exerts more force against her waist with his right hand than with his left, then the greater resulting friction force will cause her to be pushed forward in addition to the left. If she is turning to the *left* and is falling toward the right, then her partner's attempt to bring her back to the left will thrust her backward. An experienced partner will automatically accommodate for that tendency and will exert a force with his right hand toward the left *and back or front*. The first of these situations is diagrammed in figure 7.5.

An experienced ballerina will usually perform the *pirouettes* close to a balanced position so that only subtle forces are necessary from the partner. An experienced partner will be sensitive to subtle imbalances so that he can adjust the hand positions and forces quickly enough to prevent observers from noticing the problem. In fact, if the ballerina is slightly off balance to the rear, the best appearance is attained, because her partner's hands can remain slightly in back of her, shifting positions as necessary without moving in front of her in clear view of the audience. He never has to have a hand in front to pull her back, a movement that can compromise the aesthetic appearance of the *pirouette*.

Stopping Rotation

One often sees at the climax of a *pas de deux* (as in the *Nutcracker pas de deux* of Ivanov near the end of the ballet) a series of supported *pirouettes*, each multiple

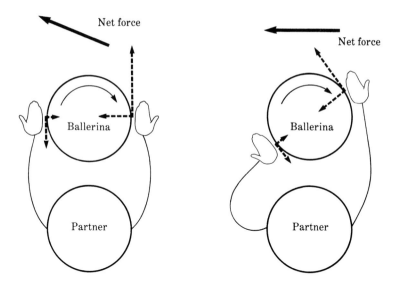

FIGURE 7.5. The supporting partner's hand positions for off-balance supported *pirouettes*, viewed from above. (left) Unbalanced to the right. (right) Unbalanced to the right, corrected.

turn ending in a pose *en face*. If the dancer remains *en pointe* at the end of the *pirouette*, there is little friction at the floor, and therefore no mechanism except her partner for getting rid of her rotational momentum. How does a partner exert the appropriate torques to stop the turn while also keeping his partner balanced?

A retarding torque to stop a *pirouette* is not difficult. Increasing the force of the hands into the waist will increase the friction force, thus slowing the turn as rapidly as desired. It is true that the ballerina helps by opening her arms as the *pirouette* ends, thereby increasing the rotational inertia and decreasing the turn rate. But the total rotational momentum is still there and must be dissipated through friction between her waist and his hands.

Clearly, a partner will find it more difficult to stop a dancer if her leg is extended while turning (as in *arabesque* or *à la seconde*) than if she is in a normal *pirouette* position with one foot at the knee of the supporting leg. One reason is that her rotational inertia is larger because more of her body mass is farther from the axis of rotation. An additional reason is the fact that the extended leg is often in his way as he tries to slow her rotation to a stop.

Although the ballerina usually finishes a turn facing the audience, sometimes the turn ends with the dancer's back to the audience, her upper back and head arched back so that her face is toward the audience. This final pose is demonstrated by Julie Kent and Benjamin Pierce in figure 7.6.

Other Supported Turns

Sometimes a turn must be initiated by a partner with a less secure contact between the two dancers than hands at the waist. It is particularly tricky when the turn must be initiated with contact only at one hand. Consider the woman in *arabesque* on her right leg, facing stage right toward her partner and maintaining balance by means of contact between her right hand and his. Suppose that from this position she must start turning to her right, bringing the free left leg from *arabesque* around to her left side (to *à la seconde*), thence into *pirouette* position with the foot at the knee of the right leg. Since she is *en pointe*, the only source of force for her to begin her rotation is her partner's hand. Now if she pushes to her left against his hand, that will certainly produce a force acting along a line some distance from the axis of rotation, and the resulting torque will indeed produce a rotation to her right. But that sideways force also will be a net force that tends to cause her to topple off balance to the right.

How does she avoid the problem of toppling caused by the same force that allows her to rotate? One technique is to exert a *twisting torque* against her partner's hand so that, although there is no net force that would tend to make her lose balance, there is a twisting torque *at the hand* that acts to cause the body to rotate. That can be difficult to carry out because, since the hands are relatively small, the twisting forces required can be very large. Remaining close to balance so that the necessary forces are small enough to be manageable is one of the challenges faced by dancers performing this movement. This is exactly the situation described in chapter 6, applied to the Rose Adagio section of *Sleeping Beauty*.

The other technique, which seems to be unconsciously applied by dancers with partnering experience, is that she makes herself lean a bit to the left just before the

FIGURE 7.6. A *pirouette* ending with the ballerina's back to the audience except for the arch in the upper body. The more common ending position is shown in the final view in figure 7.2.

start of the turn, so that, with no force against her partner's hand, she would topple to the left. Then when she does exert a force toward the left against his hand, his hand exerts the corresponding force to the right that not only produces the torque to start her turning, but also brings her back toward the balanced condition. That is a subtle adjustment for the body to make subconsciously, but experiments have shown that such an adjustment is indeed carried out. (An experiment that demonstrates that effect is to remove the partner's hand just as the woman is about to exert a force to start the turn. In most cases she does topple off balance to her left.) What is remarkable here is that the woman must anticipate the movement in a timely way and actually cause herself to be off balance in order to carry out the turn smoothly.

"Pencil" turns are another form of partnered *pirouette* from *arabesque*, this time with the partner upstage of the ballerina. Suppose she is facing stage left, with her left leg extended behind her. She brings her left leg down close to her supporting right leg while her partner exerts a torque on her waist to start her turning to her right. She gains rotational momentum and a rather large turning speed since her legs are close to the axis of rotation, which keeps her rotational inertia small. After she has turned through one or more rotations, she stops in the same *arabesque* position from which she started. Clearly, the coordinated timing is important, both to start the turn in synchronism and to stop it facing the desired direction.

Promenades are slow, controlled turns around a vertical axis on one supporting foot, often involving the partner walking around the woman so that their orientation with respect to each other remains constant. When the man walks in a circle while rotating his partner through one revolution, it is clear that he is exerting appropriate forces with his hand or hands on some part of her body to initiate the turning movement. He may have hands at her waist, or there may be hand-to-hand contact. In the latter case, the most common difficulty is maintaining her balance, which is difficult if the man moves away from or toward his partner (and her fixed axis of rotation) instead of walking in a circle. Adjustments must constantly be made in order to allow the woman to maintain an aesthetically pleasing line while maintaining balance during this promenade.

A promenade with contact between only one hand of each partner (with the woman in *attitude* position on one supporting pointed foot, for instance) looks simple, involving one dancer walking around the other while they remain facing each other. But it is difficult partly because of a problem similar to that described earlier for a *pirouette* initiated by the force from one hand of the partner. In this case, the woman must maintain her balance while rotating *and* maintain her orientation facing her partner, having only her partner's hand as a source of forces while that hand is some distance from the rotation axis. This situation was described in chapter 6 in a discussion of the Rose Adagio in *Sleeping Beauty*.

Many types of turns are supported by a partner's hands at the waist. If the rotating body were symmetric, the waist would be centered on the rotation axis, and the hands could remain in one position during the rotation. But turns almost always occur on one supporting leg, so the symmetry is broken by the fact that one foot is on the floor and the other leg is lifted. The partner must be very aware of that changing position of the waist that occurs during a rotation. An example of such a turn is a quick 180° *fouetté* turn supported by a partner's hands at the waist.

Suppose a dancer is in *arabesque* on the right supporting leg, facing stage right, as shown in the first view of figure 7.7. She brings her left leg from *arabesque* position behind her through a position close to her supporting leg and continues moving it to a position in front of her, while she remains facing stage right. When that left leg arrives at the front, she rotates her body to the right, leaving the left leg where it was, so that she ends the movement in *arabesque* facing stage left. At the beginning of the movement, her partner is holding her waist, keeping her in a balanced position. But because the mass of her leg is behind her, her waist is somewhat in front of her supporting foot. Now when her left leg moves down and through to her front, her partner must move her torso toward stage left (shifting his weight in order to do so) to prevent her from being off balance toward the right (her front) when her leg is in its new orientation. Then when the rotation begins for the half-turn, he must provide the torque and must also shift her torso toward him some distance, since the supporting leg, which was the leg closest to him, is now the leg farthest from him. These subtle shifts in where the partner's body must be held in order to maintain balance can be quite complicated and are learned by much practice. Of course a further complication is that every dancer's body is different, with different mass distribution and different ways of moving.

A Final Turn

Turns in dance are impressive movements. Partnered turns require a great deal of coordination, since the forces between partners are often quite large, and the control necessary to maintain the aesthetic image while rotating, sometimes rapidly, is

FIGURE 7.7.
A *fouetté* 180° "flip" turn from *arabesque*, as seen from the side. (The audience is to the right in the photograph.) This is a challenging movement to partner because of the coordination of the torque necessary for her turn and the changes in location of her waist when she is balanced in the three positions shown during the sequence of the total movement.

very difficult. The fact that any turning motion requires a torque from somewhere means that one challenge for the dancers is to make the turn as smooth as possible by coordinating the use of the necessary forces. Controlling both the balance and the rate of turn is another aspect that requires the cooperation of both partners. When that coordination is missing, the results are often unexpected and distracting. When these supported *pirouettes* do work, it is a tribute to the remarkable ability of the dancers to achieve that necessary coordination.

8 *The mechanics of* LIFTS

One day you were watching the impressive new man in the company working on a *pas de deux* with a woman you had often partnered in the past. The director was telling her to hold a better position in the air during the big traveling lift. "You know your leg has to stay up in the *arabesque*, and your torso and hips have to face stage right, not open facing the audience. You know better than that!"

The new man said scathingly, "Maybe I'd better find a dancer who knows what an *arabesque* is!"

That was too much. You said to the director, "It isn't her fault! May I show you what he's doing wrong?" A quick demonstration showed the woman in a perfect *arabesque* during the lift. The applause from everyone watching was a bit hard on the ego of the new man but was also an incentive for him to learn about the difficult art of partnering.

What did you do to correct the technique being used for that *arabesque* lift?

ONE DANCER LIFTING another is often seen in partnered dance. Clearly, a dancer jumping alone cannot achieve the height, the duration, or the positions possible when help from a partner is added. The intent of the lift may be to create an image of gentle floating for an ethereal creature such as Giselle or an image of defying gravity by flying through the air or simply an image of extending the range of motion beyond that possible for a single unaided dancer. The lift may represent the status implied by height, as for a queen or princess who has a lofty position relative to those around her. A lift to a position sitting on the partner's shoulder is common at the climax of a *pas de deux* in classical ballet.

The lifts described in this chapter, in which the woman is lifted by the man, are those familiar in classical ballet, although the principles can be applied to any style of dance, for any combination of genders of partners. The movements dealt with here range from low lifts, in which the woman is never very high off the ground although her weight is borne by her partner, to high overhead lifts. They range from "temporary" lifts, in which the woman is effectively performing a jump extended in time and height by the supporting force of the partner, to extended lifts, in which her weight is totally supported by the partner as she maintains a position aloft for some length of time.

The appearance of ease or difficulty in a lift may be deceptive. In Balanchine's *Theme and Variations*, for instance, there are a number of lifts, none very high but all very difficult because they require the man to lift the woman with her weight in front of him and supported there for an extended time. In the same choreographer's *Concerto Barocco*, the man carries his partner slowly across the stage for almost half a minute, alternating between an upright position in front of him and an inverted position over his back. These lifts are more difficult than they appear.

Proper technique is always important in dance, not only to allow dancers to create the desired aesthetic images but also to help avoid injury. The physical dangers are particularly great when dancers are working with partners, which requires that they coordinate movements that may involve forces, heights, and speeds not attainable by solo dancers. These dangers are particularly notable in lifts. A common problem faced by male dancers is lower-back injury resulting from the lifting re-

FIGURE 8.1. Susan Pilarre in midair between Sean Lavery and Robert Maiorano during a New York City Ballet performance of *Dances at a Gathering*, choreographed by Jerome Robbins. Martha Swope/TimePix.

quired in partnering. Women risk falling from sizable heights in partnered lifts. In fact, the danger inherent in some movements contributes to audience appeal. There is a thrill for both dancers and audiences when a woman is held 8 feet in the air with her back toward the floor, supported only by her partner's hands.

The Straight Lift

Let us start with one of the simplest lifts: a straight lift in which the woman remains vertical while her partner lifts her with his hands at her waist, from a stance directly behind her, as shown in figure 8.2. Even in this simple lift, there are several questions, potential problems, and technical dos and don'ts. There are considerations of the most effective relative sizes of the two dancers and the way they coordinate their respective motions. There is the proper technique for the woman, involving her preparation, jump, position in the air, and use of the arms. There is the proper technique for the man, involving the position of his hands, his stance behind the woman, and the muscles he uses to perform the lift. It is important for dancers to recognize that "proper" technique is not based just on style but may be physically necessary for achieving an effective and safe movement.

For proper technique in this straight lift, as in others, the lifter should delay straightening his legs until the arms are well on their way to being straight. The leg muscles are substantially stronger than the arm muscles and can be used for much of the lifting. As the arms or the legs approach full straight extension, the vertical force they can exert becomes larger. In the diagram shown in figure 8.3, the bent arm can exert only one-fourth as much lifting force as the almost fully extended arm, for the same torque at the elbow and shoulder. Therefore, the arms should be straightened vertically as much as possible while most of the upward impetus is coming from the woman's jump. As the momentum from her jump is expended, his arms and legs take over jointly for the later part of the lift. The lift then appears most smooth and flowing.

Of course, the woman must have strength also, as she must help in the lifting process by jumping and by using her arms effectively. Often the arms start at the sides, move down, and then, during push-off, rise to a position over the head. What does that movement accomplish? As we saw in chapter 3, momentum can be stored in one part of the body while forces continue to act on another part. In this case, linear vertical momentum is stored in the upward moving arms while the feet are still in contact with the floor, able to continue the push-off. The net momentum (and energy) contributed to the lift is therefore greater.

One might ask how much of the energy that goes into a lift is provided by the woman and how much by her partner. That question is easy to answer by observing how high she can jump by herself in a similar movement. If her center of gravity rises somewhat greater than 1 foot when she jumps unassisted, that height is a

FIGURE 8.2.
The highest point in a
straight lift.

measure of the work done against gravity in the jumping process, which is equal to
the increase in mechanical energy in the jump. When a partner lifts her as she contributes the same magnitude of jumping energy, her center of gravity may rise perhaps 3 feet. Since the work done, and the corresponding mechanical energy contributed to the woman's mass, are proportional to the height, the man contributes
somewhat more than half of the energy. (Recent experiments carried out at Dickinson College have verified this estimate.)

One characteristic of any lift that is very important in determining the difficulty for the lifting partner is the horizontal location of the woman's center of

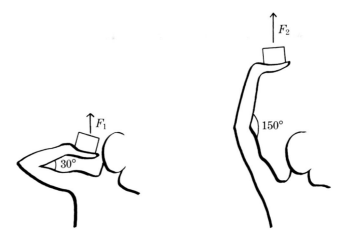

FIGURE 8.3. The difference in vertical force possible depending on arm position. When the arms are almost straight, the force is greater than when they are bent. In the case shown here, the magnitude of the force F_2 is about four times the magnitude of F_1 for the same muscle force and torque at the elbow and shoulder.

gravity relative to the location of her partner's hands on her body. If her center of gravity is located on a vertical line that passes directly between his hands, then a vertical force from his hands is all that is required to support her in the air. But if that center of gravity lies, for instance, in front of his hands when they are at her waist, then she would tend to rotate forward during the lift unless he can also exert a twisting torque to keep her oriented vertically. A common mistake made by a female dancer learning this straight-lift technique is to neglect to keep her body straight. There is a tendency to lean forward at the waist while in the air, thus displacing the center of gravity forward and making it difficult for her partner to maintain her vertical position in the air. (See figure 8.4.) A fear of the height of the lift or a desire to keep her feet away from her partner's body may motivate that flaw in body position.

To make the lift as comfortable as possible for the woman, her partner must place his hands under her rib cage. Actually, since skin and clothing do slide over the body structure to some extent, the partner must start with his hands significantly below her rib cage. One reason the wide part of a classical tutu is below the waist is to allow the partner access to the location on her body that he must utilize

THE MECHANICS OF LIFTS

FIGURE 8.4.
When Julie Kent bends at the waist in this straight lift, her center of gravity is in front of her partner's supporting hands, making the lift more difficult.

for lifts and supported *pirouettes*. And women find it more comfortable if he uses the heels of his hands more than a squeezing grip with his fingers. Finally, his stance must be sufficiently close to his partner that he is not lifting her weight too far in front of him, which would involve large torques in his shoulders and back. On the other hand, he must hold her far enough in front of him that he does not arch (hyperextend) his lower back, a position conducive to lumbar spine injury.

Why are men who often perform lifts plagued with lower-back problems? Part of the reason involves the timing of the vertical force exerted during the lift. Experiments have been carried out at Dickinson College in which force sensors were used to measure the upward force exerted by the man's hands on his partner during the straight lift described here. (The lift studied involved an ascent and immediate descent, with no time spent in a static position aloft.) Those measurements show that the force is large during the early part of the lift, smaller near the peak when he is allowing her to start to accelerate back down for the descent, then is *greatest* just before she arrives back at the floor. (See graph in figure 8.5.) Thus the greatest force he must exert occurs when his arms are low and his back is most inclined at the waist. At those times her center of gravity is farthest in front of him, requiring the greatest strain on his lower back. Why is the lifting force greatest when she is closest to the floor, particularly on the descent? One reason is that he needs to propel her upward early in the lift in order to achieve the acceleration necessary to accomplish the movement quickly. Upon descent, he is motivated to prevent injury to his partner and thus will try to cushion her descent as much as possible as she approaches the floor.

There is another reason why his muscles can exert greater force when she is descending than when she is rising, resulting from an interesting characteristic of muscle activity. Muscles can exert a large force when they are undergoing *eccentric* contraction, in which the working muscles stretch and the movement (in this case downward) is in a direction opposite to the force he is exerting. Less force is possible during *concentric* contraction, in which the muscles contract and cause movement in the same direction as the exerted force. This phenomenon is well known to those who lift weights, who recognize that they can gently lower a weight that requires help to lift. So the force the man is able to exert to support his partner is greater on the descent than on the initial ascent.

What should lifters do to alleviate the strain on the back during lifts? First, the back should be inclined as little as possible by bending the legs instead. The legs must work harder, but some of the strongest muscles in the body are the leg muscles used in the lifting process. Second, it is sometimes observed that the man will allow the woman to slide down the front of his body on descent, thereby minimizing the distance her center of gravity is in front of him and allowing him to bend his *legs* on descent rather than inclining his back. Although this technique is not as pleasing aesthetically, it may be preferable to an otherwise too rapid descent.

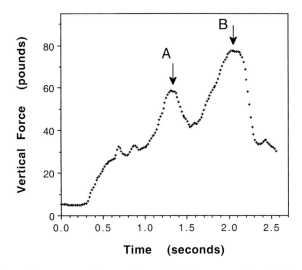

Force vs. Time for Vertical Lift

FIGURE 8.5. This graph represents the way the vertical force exerted by the lifter on his partner during a straight lift varies with time. Point A is early in the lift during ascent, and point B occurs just before the return of the lifted dancer's feet to the floor.

An impressive version of this straight lift is performed with the woman undergoing a full turn around a vertical rotation axis at the peak of the lift. In order to accomplish that more difficult feat, the upward lifting force must be sufficiently large that the woman coasts upward in free flight long enough for her partner to exert a torque at her waist and let her rotate freely between his hands. Clearly, he can exert no upward force on her while she is turning, as his hands cannot move around the circular path along with her waist. When she has completed the full turn, his hands again clamp on her waist, stopping the turn and beginning to cushion her descent. Thus, there must be enough vertical motion to perform a "throw and catch" rather than just a lift.

Other Front Lifts

Another common lift is an *arabesque* lift, in which the woman holds an *arabesque* position with one leg extended behind her and the other slightly forward of vertically beneath her while she is lifted or carried by her partner. If he is supporting her by her waist, there is a problem that can often be observed. Note that a significant part of the woman's mass is behind her when her leg is extended in *arabesque*, as shown in the first photograph in figure 8.6. In fact, if she has a good arch in her back, her upper body and lower leg can be close to vertical while the other leg is extended to the back, allowing much less of her body mass to be in front of the support from her partner's hands at her waist than in back of that support. If he exerts only an upward force at her waist, she will swing like a pendulum so that her back leg droops, her lower leg moves forward, and her upper body leans back, as seen in the second photograph in figure 8.6. That problem is prevented if the man exerts a torque on her body in addition to the supporting force—a torque that attempts to rotate her upper body forward, as Benjamin Pierce is doing in the top photograph in figure 8.6. He accomplishes that torque by moving his upper hand higher on her back and pushing forward while supporting most of her weight with his lower hand.

This problem is what you saw in the new dancer's technique described in the anecdote at the beginning of the chapter as he tried to hold his partner in the *arabesque* position during the lift. There's nothing she can do to maintain her position if he fails to provide the torque that allows her to keep her back leg lifted to horizontal. And, of course, he is responsible for the orientation of her torso in the air; *he* must keep her torso facing stage right rather than facing the audience. So your comment and demonstration showed the proper use of the hands that allows the woman to achieve the desired position.

Sometimes the desired effect for a lift is for the woman's body to appear to travel in an arching path during a traveling *grand jeté* lift, so that she starts facing somewhat upward, then rotates to an orientation facing a little downward at the end of the movement. To accomplish that, her partner must exert an even larger torque to cause her to rotate in a direction opposite to the natural tendency during the duration of the lift. This movement is shown in figure 8.7.

In another form of *arabesque* lift, the woman faces the audience on her left supporting leg with the right leg extended to the back. Her partner, also facing the audience, places his right shoulder under her right thigh. His hands support her

FIGURE 8.6.
An *arabesque* lift (top) with the appropriate forces exerted by the lifter and (bottom) with the lifter failing to apply the torque necessary, allowing the dancer to rotate out of the *arabesque* position.

FIGURE 8.7. A *grand jeté* carry, showing the gradual rotation of the dancer's orientation throughout the trajectory.

under her rib cage directly in front, and her left leg is vertical directly in front of his body. This lift is made difficult by the fact that he must start from a very low position in a deep *plié*, then straighten up with her on his shoulder. Since she starts in *arabesque* position on one supporting leg, she can provide almost no jump to help at the beginning. And he must bear a sizable part of her weight on his hands extended well in front of his body, not the easiest position from which to exert an upward force.

Overhead Lifts

Overhead lifts are impressive in that the height achieved by the woman is great, creating an expansive and grand image to the audience. There is a resulting difficulty for both partners, along with a greater danger than for smaller lifts.

A lift in which the woman is again in the *arabesque* position is the so-called press lift shown in figure 8.8. In this case Benjamin lifts Julie with his right hand below her right rib cage and his left on the thigh of her left (extended) leg. This lift can be a stable lift in which her center of gravity is directly above his shoulders and feet, with his arms straight and therefore able to exert an upward force with relative ease. There are two problems for him. One is that he receives very little help from his partner since she starts in a balanced position on one leg, often *en pointe*, not a position conducive to an effective jump. The other is that he must have sufficient flexibility in his shoulders and elbows to allow his arms to be straight overhead while his back is straight and not arched. A hyperextended curve in the lower back while supporting weight overhead is an invitation to injury!

There are other forms of overhead lifts. In one particularly impressive example, the woman, traveling or stationary in front of the man, jumps up and arches backward at the same time, while her partner, initially facing her back, lifts her with his hands on her lower back. She arrives inverted over his head, as shown in figure 8.9. In this lift, she must arch quickly enough in the process to ensure that she is presenting her partner with a lower-back "shelf" for him to lift. That is, he must be able to

FIGURE 8.8.
An *arabesque* "press" lift.

lift with the heel of his hands under her back rather than from his hands on her waist. Otherwise, when she is inverted over his head, he will be supporting her weight entirely with his thumbs, which is uncomfortable at best. And, of course, he must be supporting her weight at a position close to her center of gravity to allow her to achieve a pleasing line and to avoid rotating back in the direction from which she was lifted or rotating on over his head, which can result in an upside-down headfirst dive toward the floor, a distasteful climax to this lift! If his hands are too far up on her back, her legs will tend to be low, and she will not maintain the face-back position over his head. If his hands are too low, she will tend to rotate to a head-down position, which he can no longer control. Of course, she has some range through which she can adjust her body position so as to control the location of her center of gravity relative to the position of his supporting hands.

FIGURE 8.9.
An inverted overhead lift.

Another overhead lift, shown in the photograph of Susan Jaffe and Alexander Godunov in figure 8.10, is the "angel lift," in which the woman arrives over the man's head facing down with her back arched. In the usual preparation, she runs toward her partner in order to create some momentum that can contribute to the lift (much as a pole-vaulter converts horizontal momentum to vertical momentum in order to clear the bar). He must then lift her with his hands near the front of her hip bones, slowing her forward momentum with an appropriate horizontal force as he lifts and controls her ascent to the overhead position, where she usually faces the audience while he faces away. Again, if his hands are too high, she will fall back in the direction from which she was lifted, while if they are too low, she might continue on over his head. In any case, the woman must hold her position with a strong back, or her partner's job becomes impossibly difficult.

In a more impressive lift similar to that just described, the woman is suspended horizontally on her side by the hand of her partner's arm extended vertically above him. Note that this lift is possible only if the woman's center of gravity, which in equilibrium must be directly over his supporting hand, is very close to her hip bone, as that structural part of her body is the only comfortable place for her weight to be supported when she's horizontal. A woman with too long or too short a torso might find this lift impossible.

The descent from high lifts can be as difficult to control as the ascent. From these overhead lifts, control of the aesthetic line must be maintained by both partners during the descent, a task not easily accomplished at the same time as the necessary slowing of the descent that cushions the landing. From the inverted overhead lift, for instance, there is a strong temptation for the woman to bend forward on descent so that she can see the floor that she is approaching. But, in order to maintain the line, she must trust that her partner will place her down gently at just the right moment and position.

Other Lifts

Some other lifts are worth noting. The "Bluebird" lift is named for a movement in the Bluebird *pas de deux* from *Sleeping Beauty*. In this lift (to her partner's *right* shoulder, for example) the woman approaches the man face-to-face, kicks her left leg in front of her just to her partner's right side, then jumps up and rotates to a horizontal position front-side-down (as in a *tour jeté*). She lands on his right shoulder, arching her back so as to face the audience, as shown in figure 8.11. Her partner's job is to guide her up to his shoulder with his right hand on her back and his left hand holding her left hand. This lift is quite beautiful and is relatively easy if the timing and takeoff motion are correct. But she can easily land on his shoulder with her weight too far forward, tending to fall headfirst in front of him, or with her weight too far back, in which case she might continue past him and land on her feet in back of him. If her weight is too far from his neck, the strain on his shoulder can be extreme. The descent from this lift can actually be more challenging than the lift, since he must support her weight on bent knee as she descends from full height.

In many *pas de deux*, the woman ends sitting on the man's shoulder with one leg bent toward the audience and the other bent down in front of him, both dancers facing the audience, as Benjamin and Julie demonstrate in figure 8.12. In this "shoulder sit" the man lifts the woman by the waist (she helps by jumping) and places her on his shoulder. One problem that sometimes occurs in this lift is that the woman waits too long before assuming a sitting position, and the man has no horizontal surface that he can put on his shoulder. That is, if her legs remain vertical as he tries to put her on his shoulder, they run into his chest, and she ends up "sitting" on his chest rather than his shoulder. He must then lean back and use his hands to

FIGURE 8.11.
The "Bluebird" lift.

push her back against his body to keep her from falling off. The position is not the most graceful.

A shoulder sit can also culminate from a preparation in which the woman runs toward the man, then jumps and turns into a sitting position simultaneously as he lifts and guides her onto his shoulder. Problems in that movement may involve a jump that continues moving horizontally so that he has difficulty getting rid of her traveling momentum, or a misjudgment of landing position so that she misses his shoulder.

Some lifts require a greater degree of strength and coordination from both partners and are thus more impressive. One is a lift from the ballet *Spring Waters*,

FIGURE 8.12.
A "shoulder sit" often seen at
the end of a *pas de deux*.

choreographed by Asaf Messerer. The woman stands on her right foot with the left
bent so its foot is at the right knee. The man, standing behind and to her left, pre-
pares to lift her left ankle with his left hand, while his right hand is placed at her
buttocks so that she can sit on it when aloft. She jumps from her right leg, pushes
down with her left leg by straightening it while he lifts that leg, and she bends her
right leg up, reaching a position supported by his right hand under her right buttock
at the top of his straight right arm, left leg extended down vertically. This lift is impressive partly because her head and arms reach a greater height than in any other
partnered dance movement.

Catches

In the lifts described here, the lifter provides at least part of the upward force that elevates the lifted dancer. Catches may involve a jump by one dancer, the other catching her near the highest point in the movement. Such movements appear smoothest when the catch is made exactly at the peak of the trajectory, for two reasons. First, at the time the jumper is at the peak, the vertical velocity is zero. If that height is maintained after the catch, the trajectory follows a smooth path, since the vertical velocity smoothly approaches zero and then remains zero after the catch. If the catch is made after the descent has begun, the downward motion must be stopped. Second, if the catch is at the peak, the force exerted by the catcher is never greater than the weight of the lifted dancer, whereas if she is caught during descent, he must exert sufficient vertical force not only to support her weight but also to decelerate the descent to a zero vertical velocity. Conversely, if the catch occurs *before* the peak, the free-flight phase of the movement is truncated, making it less impressive.

An example of a catch is a "*tour jeté* catch," in which the woman approaches the man face-to-face, as in the Bluebird lift described earlier. She approaches his left side, jumps from her left foot, kicks her right leg up, rotates in the air, then reverses her legs so that her right leg approaches the vertical below her (or is bent with the foot at the knee of the left leg), and her left leg is extended to her rear. Her partner catches her with his right hand or arm at her ribs while his left catches her left leg as it rises toward horizontal. When performed smoothly, the impression is one of a traveling jump with a turn at the peak, smoothly stopping suspended at that highest point. The upward thrust is provided totally by the jumper; the catcher merely stops her vertical motion in midair.

A Final Thrust

The lifts and catches described here represent ways in which a dancer can, with the aid of a partner, create movements far beyond those possible alone. Some of the lifts are simple straight lifts, in which we can see reasons for technical problems often observed, and reasons for vulnerability to injury associated with these movements. Larger overhead lifts are impressive but require careful timing and location of supporting forces in order to produce the image of smoothness and lightness desired. Catches create a different image than lifts; a dancer's expected trajectory through the air is suspended at its peak through the intervention of a partner.

Moving through the air or hovering several feet off the floor is impressive to do and to watch. These aesthetic images can be accomplished only by dancers who have the necessary skill, training, strength, and trust in a partner to perform them safely and with a smoothness that belies the effort involved.

9   *The effects of*

BODY SIZE

You were nearing the end of your fourth class of the day, doing the expected *grand allegro* with big energetic jumps traveling diagonally across the studio. As usual, the teacher had asked the pianist to slow down the music for you and the other men so that, with your larger bodies, you could jump to the height you were capable of, rather than being constrained by the faster music appropriate for the smaller female dancers. You noticed that the other men looked as exhausted as you did at the end of that class. Why didn't the women look as tired? Were they just in better shape?

Then you realized there was a good reason why the men should feel more drained than the women! What is your insight?

THE TALLER MAN has a distinct advantage when partnering tall women, but height can be a disadvantage for other types of movement. Adagio movements may appear smoother when performed by a tall person, but allegro movements require considerably more strength than the same movements performed by shorter dancers at the same tempo.

Dance teachers are particularly aware of differences between children and adults in the performance of dance movement. Although adults often have better-developed muscles, greater coordination, and increased understanding, one often notices children performing certain types of movements more easily. Dance students undergoing a growth spurt in their early teen years usually experience a temporary loss of grace and body coordination. And choreographers are often aware that they must have different expectations of large and small dancers in terms of line, music tempo, and general style of movement.

Are there physical analyses that can help us understand the reasons for these effects of size on movement? It is well known that accelerating a large mass requires a larger force than changing the velocity of a small mass at the same rate. But some of the more subtle "scaling" problems are not so obvious.

Why is it that vertical jumps with beats of the legs, or scissoring movements that separate the legs and then bring them together again (*entrechats quatre, entrechats six*, etc.), are more difficult for taller dancers? Why is it that tall dancers have more difficulty pointing their feet when they clear the ground in vertical jumps? How much more strength does the tall dancer require to perform the same movements as the shorter dancer in the same tempo? What special problems do horizontal accelerations and *pirouettes* present for the larger dancer?

Height of a Vertical Jump

First let us consider vertical jumps. Much of this analysis applies to any jumps, whether in ballet, modern dance, or even activities other than dance. Often dance choreography calls for vertical motion *and* beats with the legs while in the air. We

will deal with the vertical motion first and then the beats. In chapter 3 the relationship between time in the air and the height of a jump was discussed. We saw that the height of a jump is strongly related to the duration of the jump as determined by the music tempo, making dancers particularly sensitive to that tempo.

One implication of the relationship between time and height for a jump is that dancers of different sizes must jump the same absolute height off the floor in order to perform similar movements to the same tempo. If the tempo is slow, the shorter dancer may not be able to jump sufficiently high to "fill" the music, which leads to an apparent jerkiness. But another aspect of the jump creates a *disadvantage* for the tall dancer. Part of an observer's impression of the height of a jump depends on that height *relative to the dancer's height*. That is, for a jump taking half a second in

FIGURE 9.1.
Dancers large and small, in a scene from New York City Ballet's *Nutcracker*. Martha Swope/TimePix.

the air, the jump height of about 1 foot may be one-fourth of the body height of a short dancer but only one-sixth of the body height of a tall dancer. Such a jump by a tall dancer just does not look as impressive. Again, there is nothing the tall dancer can do to extend his jump height without taking a longer time and lagging behind the music.

Suppose Sean Lavery, who is over 6 feet tall, has an understudy (the author's daughter) who is 5 feet 3 inches tall and who is attempting the same choreography, as shown in figure 9.2. In this case the taller Sean jumps to about the same proportion of his height as the shorter Virginia (in the second photo) but clearly, as shown in the last view, arrives back at the floor later than the shorter dancer.

Now let's consider the strength required to support or move a larger body. We've all noticed how a skinny-legged spider easily carries more than its own weight, or how a flea is able to jump many times its own height, whereas the fat legs of an elephant hardly do more than support the animal's weight against gravity. The reason for the difference can be understood by imagining two geometrically similar animals, such as a rat and a mouse, both of which we will assume have exactly the same shape (the same body proportions), but one is twice as large as the other in each linear dimension: height, width, and length. The volume, and hence the mass, of the body is proportional to the third power of the linear dimension; the rat thus has a weight eight times that of the mouse. But the cross-sectional area of the legs supporting the body depends only on the second power of the linear dimension, so that the rat has only four times the leg area of the mouse. Thus the rat is supporting eight times the weight on four times the area, resulting in double the stress or pressure on the leg structure.

Excess stress or pressure on the body is responsible for injuries, which is one reason small people suffer fewer injuries. Of course, young people of any size have more flexibility in bones and tissues, which contributes to their resilience and affords some protection from injury.

An important effect of size is the force a muscle can exert, which is roughly proportional to the cross sectional area of the total packet of fibers in a particular muscle. If our rat has muscles twice the linear size of the mouse's, the muscles would have four times the cross-sectional area and could exert four times the force. But if the mass to be accelerated is eight times as great, the rat is going to have more difficulty in its movements and must exert more muscular effort to accelerate at the same rate as the mouse.

How do these scaling principles apply to dancers? Suppose a young male dancer is, like Virginia, 5 feet 3 inches tall, while Sean is just over 6 feet (15 percent taller). Further, suppose their bodies are identically shaped (same proportions). Sean will weigh about 52 percent more than Shorty and will have muscles 32 percent stronger (because they are 32 percent greater in cross-sectional area). Thus, in order to jump to a height of 1 foot, taking 0.5 second, Sean must exert 15 percent more muscular effort. Alternatively, in order to jump to a height of about one-fifth of his own height (a 1 foot jump for Shorty), Sean must jump about 1.2 feet and exert 32 percent more muscular effort than the shorter dancer.

Consider the energy required for this movement, which is directly related to the number of calories burned in the process of moving the body. The physical work done in a vertical jump is the product of the weight and the height and thus is 52 percent more for Sean than for Shorty, if both jump to the same height. If each dancer jumps to the same *proportion of his own height*, Sean expends about 75 percent more energy! These relationships apply in varying degrees to all kinds of movement, and dancers of different sizes have learned to adjust to the expectations placed upon them. But fatigue does depend to some extent on the total expenditure of energy, and large dancers sometimes have to expend *much* larger magnitudes of energy than smaller dancers in order to carry out similar moves.

Your experience in class described in the opening anecdote now makes sense. The slowing of the music allows the men to jump closer to the same proportion of their own height as the smaller women, which, in the numerical example above, means that they expend 75 percent more energy than the smaller dancers! No wonder it is difficult for larger men to keep up the same schedule of dance classes as smaller dancers.

Entrechats

Now let us consider the beats with the legs that Sean must perform while in the air during his jump. These beats are oscillating rotations of the leg around a horizontal axis through the hip joint. A torque is required at the hip in order to produce the rotational acceleration (see appendix B). In order for *entrechats* to be accomplished in the same tempo by both Sean and Shorty, and with the same angular amplitude (perhaps oscillating through an arc of 10°), the rotational accelerations of the legs will be the same for both of them. As shown in appendix B, the torque required is proportional to the rotational inertia, which depends not only on the mass but on the square of the distance of the mass from the rotation axis. (The contributions from the many small individual parts of the leg, at their respective distances from the rotation axis at the hip, must be added.) The mass of each comparable fraction of the total leg volume is 52 percent greater for Sean; the square of the distance to the hip joint for each such increment of mass is 32 percent greater

FIGURE 9.2.
A short and a tall dancer jumping to a height that is about the same proportion of their own height. Here the author's daughter Virginia substitutes for Sean Lavery's "understudy" and arrives at the floor before Sean, who jumped higher.

for Sean. So the rotational inertia of a leg is proportional to the fifth power of its linear size and is 101 percent greater for Sean than Shorty, and Sean must exert *double the torque* to produce the same rotational acceleration and hence the same leg motion in the same tempo!

Other factors make the problem less severe. Sean's muscles, being 32 percent larger in cross-sectional area, can exert 32 percent more force for the same "effort." And the structure of the joint, including the distance from the center of the joint to the point of muscle attachment to the bone, is also bigger in Sean. This allows a particular muscle force to produce more torque. The final result is that Sean must still exert 32 percent more muscular "effort" to perform beats at the same rate and same amplitude as his smaller counterpart!

How about the energy expended doing *entrechats*? Since the angular movement is assumed to be the same for the different bodies, the energy required is proportional to the torque. Thus Sean is expending energy at about *double* the rate of Shorty!

Horizontal Accelerations and Body Size

Suppose a dancer must undergo a quick horizontal acceleration away from his initial position. As we have seen in chapter 3, this acceleration is proportional to the horizontal friction force between the foot and the floor, and inversely proportional to the body's mass. Since the friction force is proportional to the weight, there is no advantage or disadvantage associated with size in realizing sufficient nonslipping friction force to accomplish a particular linear acceleration.

But how does the dancer achieve the off-balance condition necessary for a horizontal force and acceleration? These techniques, discussed in chapter 3, do involve slower processes for larger dancers. For instance, the toppling of the body from a vertical configuration to one of increasing angle with the vertical makes it possible to exert an increasing horizontal accelerating force against the floor. But the rate of topple is slower in direct proportion to the linear size. So it will take longer for a tall dancer to "topple" to a sufficient angle to exert the required horizontal accelerating force against the floor—15 percent longer for Sean than for Shorty.

Body Size and Pirouettes

Does a tall dancer experience a disadvantage or advantage compared with a shorter person in performing a *pirouette?*

The rotational inertia of a body around any axis of rotation depends on the fifth power of the linear size of the body (assuming the same shape for bodies of different sizes). So Sean's rotational inertia around a vertical axis is double that of Shorty. Sean can exert 32 percent more force with his muscles (which are that much larger in cross-sectional area than Shorty's). The horizontal forces of the feet against the floor, which produce the force couple that initiates the *pirouette*, are thus 32 percent greater for Sean. However, the same body position will produce a 15 percent larger distance between front and back feet in the preparatory position, so the accelerating torque will be 52 percent greater for Sean than for Shorty. But we're then left with a rotational acceleration 32 percent less for Sean than for Shorty, or else Sean must exert 32 percent more muscular effort than Shorty in order to perform the *pirouettes* at the same rate.

The frictional force at the floor is a problem. When the shoe is not moving against the floor, the horizontal force between the two surfaces can be as great as $F = CW$, where C is the coefficient of static friction, and W is the body weight. (Note that the force does not depend on the surface area of contact.) Thus for a given coefficient of friction the friction force can be as much as 52 percent greater for Sean than for Shorty. The greater spread of feet in the preparatory position means that the torque can be as much as 75 percent greater for Sean. But in order to produce the same rotational acceleration as Shorty, Sean must exert 101 percent greater torque. Thus, the larger dancer may require a larger coefficient of friction —requiring more rosin, for instance—to perform *pirouettes* at the same rate as a smaller dancer. Slipping of the feet at the beginning of a *pirouette* can be more of a problem for Sean than for Shorty.

Adagio Movements

Most of the effects of size discussed here result in disadvantages for the larger dancer. It is true, however, that slow movements sometimes look more graceful and smooth when performed by taller people.

One reason for the smoothness of movement common for taller dancers involves the slower accelerations that result from the muscular effort of a large person. When Sean exerts 90 percent of his strength in a particular movement, his body responds with a corresponding acceleration. Shorty, to produce movement at the same rate, will exert perhaps 50 percent of his strength. It is probably easier to control the body smoothly when the exertion required is close to zero or close to maximum, and hardest halfway between. For example, if Sean is exerting 90 percent of his possible force, he has a range of only an additional 10 percent between his existing force and the maximum he can exert. Shorty, on the other hand, has a range of forces up to double his existing force before he reaches his maximum; a variation of 10 percent within that broad range may be difficult to feel and control. Thus,

Shorty will have more difficulty moving smoothly at the slow tempo, which requires less of his strength.

Body Size and Partnered Dance

Dancers need to be able to work with partners large and small, strong and weak. There are obvious advantages for a strong male working with a small, light woman. But there are some unexpected insights that arise from careful consideration of the effects of size.

Partnered dance often involves lifts, which require both timing and strength from the lifter. Consider two dancers to be lifted. One, if 2 inches taller and the same geometrical shape as the other, will weigh about 10 percent more, or 110 pounds compared to 100 pounds. The strong dependence of weight on height results from the third-power relationship discussed earlier. Of course, body shape, density, and strength are very important considerations, making the quantitative analysis somewhat crude.

Body height also has a *direct* effect on the difficulty of a lift. A shorter woman may be lighter, but also the part of her body her partner is actually lifting will be closer to the floor at the beginning of the lift. Now the vertical force that the lifter can exert depends greatly on his position and the height of his hands. When the hands are low, it is difficult to exert as much upward force. Not only is his back inclined at the hip, with a resulting strain on the lumbar spine, but it is more difficult to exert a force with the legs when the knees are bent more than 90°. When the hands are chest high, a great deal of weight can be supported. The force decreases as the bent arms support the weight, then reaches another maximum when the arms are straight overhead.

The lifter is thus least able to lift effectively when the movement starts and the woman is close to the floor. If she does not have the strength for a strong jump to contribute to the lift, the lifter faces a harder job with a short woman than with a taller one.

Now suppose a male dancer is partnering a woman *en pointe* on one leg, so that he is responsible for her balance. As we have seen before, he maintains her balance through horizontal forces from his hands on her waist. Suppose she is off balance toward her right by 10°; that is, her center of gravity is on a line through the support at the floor that makes an angle of 10° with the vertical. Her partner detects that she is off balance by feeling the horizontal force on his right hand. But that force is proportional to her weight. Male dancers say that it can be harder to partner a very light woman because it is harder to detect when she is off balance, and she can be leaning quite far before he is aware. Of course, once he is aware, it is easier to return her to balance, but that might be too late for her to accomplish her movement smoothly.

The same analysis applies to turns. All forces used to detect the position or condition of the woman, and all forces used to change the state of motion of the woman, are proportional to the woman's weight. There *can* be disadvantages to working with a very light woman.

Effects of Body Shape

In these analyses of scaling factors, it was assumed that bodies of different sizes have the *same shape*, or body proportions. It is probably true, however, that a dancer 15 percent taller than another is less than 15 percent larger in the lateral dimensions. Many of these analyses would have to be changed slightly if the assumption of same shape were indeed *not* valid. Some of the disadvantages of height would be less severe. However, it is interesting to note that if the larger person were relatively less broad in the lateral dimensions (more slender in shape), one would have to assume also that the cross-sectional area of the muscles was larger by *less than* the second power of the linear dimension. Some of the compensating factors would disappear, and the disadvantage of size would remain!

A Final Comparison

These results are summarized in table 9.1, which lists the various body and movement characteristics and the percentage by which each is greater for Sean, a 6 foot

Table 9.1 Percentage by which certain body characteristics or movements are greater for a 6 ft 1/2 in dancer than for a 5 ft 3 in dancer

Height	15%
Weight	52%
Cross-sectional area of supporting legs	32%
Cross-sectional area of muscles (and therefore muscle strength for a given "muscular effort")	32%
Height of jump in a specific time interval	same
Energy required for jump to same height	52%
Energy required for jump to same proportion of body height	75%
Rotational inertia around any rotation axis	101%
Torque required for a particular rotational acceleration around any axis	101%
Muscular effort for a particular rotational acceleration: *entrechats* or *pirouettes*	32%

1/2 inch dancer, than for Shorty, a 5 foot 3 inch dancer with exactly the same shape, or body proportions, as Sean.

What are the disadvantages and advantages for a tall dancer compared with a short one, then? First, for the same time in the air determined by the tempo of the music, the taller person may have trouble completing the movement in the allotted time with pointed feet, since the height of the jump is the same, independent of body shape or size. Second, the appearance of elevation in a jump depends somewhat on the height of the jump *relative to the height of the person*. The tall person does not appear to be jumping as high in the same length of time as the shorter person. But the energy required is significantly greater for the taller person.

The difficulty of executing beats with the legs while in the air is strongly dependent on body size. And because the inertia associated with the mass of a larger person determines the acceleration produced by a given force, horizontal accelerations are more difficult for larger dancers.

Since the torque required to produce a particular rate of turn is proportional to the body's rotational inertia, and the rotational inertia depends drastically on body size (*double* for a dancer 15 percent taller), the difficulty of executing smooth *pirouettes* is compounded with increasing size.

One advantage that larger dancers have is a greater smoothness in performing adagio movements, because the movements require a greater proportion of their available strength. And some of the problems in other movements may be less severe because taller dancers are generally not as much larger in lateral dimensions as in height.

What can the tall dancer do about some of these problems? Awareness of the reasons for the problems is the first step. Problems involving horizontal forces against the floor can be alleviated by the use of rosin on the floor or moisture on the shoes. The larger dancer must also learn to *anticipate* movements, starting to exert the necessary forces earlier than smaller dancers.

Sometimes larger dancers are observed carrying out quick movements as well as small dancers. Recognizing the difficulty of that feat, an observer may be able to distinguish between the use of pure strength and the use of adjustments in technique. In companies with dancers of widely varying sizes, wise artistic directors are very conscious of the differences in movement styles appropriate to the different sizes. The analyses carried out here give a more quantitative idea of the causes and magnitudes of those differences, showing that in some types of movement the effects of size are far greater than in others.

10   *A step into the future*

There you were, just past your eleventh birthday, knowing you could perform the movement the choreographer was yelling for. The older, taller dancers just couldn't stay with the music when doing their *entrechats six*. But the choreographer, knowing you were not as strong or experienced as the others, was convinced you could not possibly perform this challenging move.

Finally, you worked up your nerve to say to her, "I can make this work, and here's why!" The choreographer, intrigued that a child was going to explain something technical to her, listened as you explained why a smaller person would be able to do this movement despite having less muscular strength than the more experienced, larger dancers. Her flustered expression became a raised eyebrow and skeptical smile as she said, "Well, give it a try!" She then watched in amazement as you performed the *entrechats six* with ease, exactly on the music.

What did you explain to the choreographer?

WHAT WILL DANCERS be doing in twenty years? What will artists in other fields be doing—or scientists, for that matter? No one knows, because any creative activity, whether art or science, depends on the unpredictable imaginations of the practitioners of those activities. And where does one find the most imaginative and unfettered thinking? In our young people!

In many fields of human activity, including science and the arts, there are those who feel that the remaining opportunities for creative innovation are limited—that everything interesting that can be done has already been done. Where are innovations still occurring in science? What role do science and its cousin technology play in the continuing evolution of the arts?

In science, true advances are increasingly difficult. As understanding of nature is sought at deeper and deeper levels, the instruments necessary become larger and larger, and increasingly expensive. The superconducting supercollider, now unfulfilled history, was designed to investigate the tiniest and most fundamental building blocks of all matter. But it would have cost billions of dollars and covered an area the size of a large city. Our society made a conscious decision: such progress in understanding the most fundamental aspects of nature is just too costly. Currently, most research produces small increments of advance in the total body of knowledge. But there is always hope among scientists that they can be clever enough to solve some of the remaining major puzzles of nature.

In music, major innovations no longer seem possible within the traditional context of straightforward harmonic, melodic, and rhythmic structures familiar to our ears. Advances in music composition have involved more and more extensive departures from the easily understood and appreciated structures. But progress in music also occurs through the use of technology. Electronics and computer technology have provided both composers and performers with tools that are beyond the wildest dreams of musicians even a few decades ago. The range of tones, combinations, textures, and rhythms accessible to musicians is now limited only by the ability of the human ear to perceive and interpret.

What are the constraints on the future evolution of human physical activity—athletics and dance? Are there ways in which science or technology can alleviate

those constraints for dance as they have for music? One cannot avoid the fact that the fundamental instrument of dance and athletics is the human body, which cannot be changed in major ways by technical means. It is true that an understanding of anatomy can help dancers and athletes maximize the effectiveness with which their bodies perform. And such understanding can help the medical profession minimize the vulnerability of dancers and athletes to injury.

Athletes, like dancers, continually strive to maximize the effectiveness of their performance. Sometimes technology contributes a major advance, such as the invention of the fiberglass pole-vault pole. Occasionally a fundamentally new technique for an athletic activity is invented, such as the "Fosbury flop" for the high jump. But in this case also, a technological advance—the air bag used to cushion the landing—made that new high-jump technique feasible.

How are science and technology contributing to the advancement of dance?

FIGURE 10.1. Young people, like these at the Dance Theatre of Harlem, are the future of dance, both for aesthetic creativity and for their openness to understanding the principles that govern how they can move.

The development of systems for notating and recording dance for historical and archival purposes complement innovation in the creation of dance. These systems, aided by video and computer technology, allow for otherwise ephemeral dances to be retained for the future. Such archives are necessary, since newness is empty without the record of tradition from which it grows. It is also true that computer simulations are beginning to help choreographers develop their craft efficiently, without the need to have live dancers available throughout their experimentation.

Technology can be a tool for making choreographers' and dancers' jobs easier. Science, on the other hand, produces new and deeper levels of understanding of the activity of dance itself. The natural structure of physical law is the framework in which the dancer and choreographer create movement. That is, not every imaginable movement is possible within the constraints of human anatomy or of physical law. Movement conceived by the choreographer and implemented by the dancer is most effective when those constraints are well understood. For then those limitations emerge as a framework that is an integral part of the beauty of dance movement.

There is a great need for people from the worlds of science and dance to build bridges between their areas. In that way there can be growth in the contributions that science can make to dance. Scientists need to grasp the context in which their science can be useful; people in the dance world must be open to the value of the understanding that science can provide.

Who in the dance community represents that openness most vividly? Our youth! There has long been a tendency for adults to underestimate the ability of young people to understand the concepts of science. This misjudgment results both from the anxiety about science shared by many adults and from the mistaken idea that a lack of mathematical sophistication translates inherently into a lack of scientific insight. The ability of young dancers to understand the science behind what they do has been demonstrated repeatedly for those who give them a chance.

Our eleven-year-old in the anecdote at the beginning of this chapter just might have been the only one in the group who recognized that it takes *much* less effort to cause a slightly smaller leg to oscillate around the hip joint than a larger leg. In fact, the smaller person can perform those *entrechats six* rapidly despite having less muscle strength because the inertial resistance of the smaller leg to such oscillations is so much less.

The aim of this book has been to help build that physical framework within which dance movement exists. We know that the basic physical principles are sound and do indeed apply to the human body. The challenge is to make an understanding of this framework not a mere abstraction but *useful* in a way that contributes to improvement in dance technique and to an appreciation of the beauty of dance.

Appendix A
Linear Mechanics and Newton's Laws

MECHANICS" IS THE study of the properties of motion of massive objects in response to forces acting on them. The description of motion itself is "kinematics," involving relationships between position, velocity, acceleration, and time. "Dynamics" involves the relationships between motion and the causes of changes in the state of motion. A deeper treatment of mechanics can be found in any college-level introductory physics textbook.

Kinematics

Position is a description of the location of a point representing a particle or some specified point in an extended object. Position can be described in one dimension (along a line such as the vertical line important in describing the characteristics of vertical jumps or lifts), two dimensions (as in defining location on a stage floor or the trajectory of a jump in a vertical plane), or three dimensions (necessary for describing jumps moving around a stage area).

Velocity is the rate of change of position, given by the distance traveled divided by the time required, and directed from the earlier position to the later. For instance, a dancer moving 15 feet from upstage center to downstage center in 3 seconds has a velocity of 5 feet per second toward downstage. Speed is just the magnitude of velocity, with no direction specified. The speed of that dancer would be just 5 feet per second.

Acceleration is the rate of change of velocity, given by the difference between a later velocity and an earlier velocity, divided by the time required for the change. Note that an acceleration results from a change in the magnitude of the velocity *or* from a change in its direction. If the dancer moving downstage at 5 feet per second slows to a stop in one second, the acceleration would be 5 feet per second *per second*, directed *upstage*. If the dancer moving downstage *reverses* his velocity, so that he is then moving upstage at 5 feet per second, and this reversal takes one second, the acceleration is 10 feet per second *per second*. Note that the speed is 5 feet per second before and after the acceleration, but the velocity has changed significantly because the direction of motion has changed. As we will see later, any change in velocity requires a force.

A special case of changing direction of velocity is motion at a constant speed in a circle. That motion is accelerated toward the center of the circle because of the constantly changing direction of velocity, even if the motion stays at a constant radius from the center (and a constant speed).

Several useful relationships, called the "kinematic" equations, can be derived which relate the quantities that describe motion: distance, velocity, acceleration, and time. These relationships will allow us to relate time of flight to height of a jump, and to calculate the forces required for certain movements. For simplicity, let us consider motion in one dimension only, thus avoiding the need to use vectors. The simplest of these relationships is

$$s = vt,$$

where v is the average velocity during the time t taken to travel the distance s. Acceleration and velocity are related by

$$v_2 - v_1 = at,$$

where a is the average acceleration during the time t it takes to change the velocity from v_1 to v_2. Other useful relationships are

$$v_2{}^2 - v_1{}^2 = 2as$$

and

$$s = \left(\frac{1}{2}\right)at^2.$$

From this last equation we can derive a relationship between the height of a jump and the time in the air. A body acted upon by no forces other than gravity (a "free-fall" condition) will accelerate downward at a constant acceleration called g, which has a numerical value of 32 feet per second per second for any mass. In the above equation, let t be the time during which the body is accelerating downward from its highest point; s, the distance from the highest point to the ground; and a, the acceleration due to gravity, g. Solving for t produces the equation

$$t = \sqrt{2s/g}.$$

Recognizing that s is just the height of the jump H, and that it takes the same length of time to slow to a stop while rising as it takes to accelerate back down to the floor, we have the equation relating the *total time in the air* T to the height of a jump:

$$T = 2\sqrt{2H/g}.$$

A jump 1 foot high will thus produce a time in the air of 1/2 second for *any* body.

The preceding discussions have dealt with kinematics, or relationships between the variables that describe motion. Let us turn now to *dynamics*, or analyses of motions of bodies in response to forces.

Dynamics

Isaac Newton's three laws of motion, which he developed in the seventeenth century, form the basis of essentially all of classical dynamics. They can be stated as follows:

Newton's First Law: In the absence of any interaction with the rest of the universe, a body will either remain at rest or move in a straight line with a constant velocity.

Newton's Second Law: If a force *F* is applied to a body of mass *m*, the resulting acceleration *a* is given by $a = F/m$.

Newton's Third Law: If body 1 exerts on body 2 a force F_{12}, then body 2 exerts a force on body 1 of F_{21} that is equal in magnitude but opposite in direction to F_{12}.

Some examples of the application of these laws will be useful. Although it usually takes some force to keep an object moving, that force is necessary only to overcome unavoidable friction or drag forces that act in a direction opposing the motion. A dancer moving across a floor will move in a straight line at constant speed unless there is some external force acting to change the dancer's state of motion. That force may be the floor or another dancer.

Circular motion is motion with a constantly changing direction. Since the velocity is changing, there is an acceleration, and a force is necessary to produce that acceleration. If you whirl a ball around your head on the end of a string, you must exert an inward force on the string to keep the ball moving in its curved path. A dancer moving in a circular path must have a force exerted on him by the floor similar to that of the string, again directed toward the center of the circular motion, as shown in the diagram figure A.1.

The second law relates the magnitude of the force to the resulting acceleration. A heavy person (large weight and mass) requires a larger force to cause a change in velocity at a certain rate than a small person. Let us consider two falling objects,

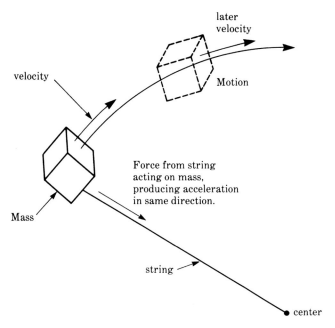

velocity

later
velocity

Motion

Force from string
acting on mass,
producing acceleration
in same direction.

Mass

string

center

FIGURE A.I. This diagram shows the centripetal force toward the center of a circular path, which keeps the mass moving in its curved path.

one more massive than the other. The gravitational field of the earth produces a downward vertical force on each object. This force, called the weight, is proportional to the body's mass. However, although the downward force on the heavy body is greater, the inertial mass that limits the acceleration is also greater. So the larger mass has a greater gravitational force acting on it, but that greater force is just enough to accelerate the larger mass with the same acceleration as for the smaller mass. As a result, the downward acceleration, g, due to the gravitational force is the same for all bodies and is numerically equal to 32 feet per second per second. Thus, in the absence of the force of air resistance, all objects would accelerate in free fall at the same rate and would take the same time to fall a given distance. This result was supposedly demonstrated by Galileo in the well-known story of two objects dropped from the Leaning Tower of Pisa.

The third law is very important in dance, as any accelerations require forces exerted on the body, and the body is exerting equal and opposite forces on the agent of the accelerating force. That is, if a dancer wishes to accelerate toward the front of a stage, he must exert a force against the stage to the rear, and the stage will then exert the equal and opposite forward accelerating force on the dancer. A common question among beginning students of physics is "How can there be any acceleration of a body if any force is balanced by an equal and opposite force?" The answer is that those equal and opposite forces are acting on different things: the floor and the dancer. There is still an unbalanced force *on the dancer's body*, causing *it* to accelerate. (Actually, the response of the stage and earth attached to it is also an acceleration, in this case undetectably small because of the large mass of the earth.)

What forces are exerted on a person standing at rest on a floor? Since the body is not accelerating, the sum of all forces acting on the body must be zero. Earth's gravity exerts a downward force that effectively acts at the center of gravity of the body, and the floor exerts a vertical upward force on the body through the feet. The body exerts an equal downward force on the floor.

Now consider the forces acting on the upper part of the body, above the waist. The gravitation of the earth exerts a force downward on the upper body that is equal to the weight of that portion of the body (perhaps half of the total weight). That force is balanced by an upward force exerted by the lower body on the upper body. There are no other forces acting on the upper body as a whole, so that a compressive force must exist in the body at the waist, no matter whether one is "placed," "pulled up," or incorrectly aligned. In fact, since the internal organs of the body can support little compressive force, most of that force is effectively borne by the spine. The compressive force in the spine is a maximum at the base of the spine, because there is more of the body weight to be supported above that point than above a higher point. Of course, at the feet the entire body's weight must be supported by a compressive force exerted on what may be a small area of the foot on *demi-pointe* or *pointe*.

Suppose now that a partner is lifting a dancer by the waist. If the dancer is suspended motionless aloft, the lifting force exerted by the partner must equal the dancer's weight. But for the lifted person, that force is no longer a compressive force at the feet. The lower half of the body is now suspended with extension, or stretching, forces, while the upper body remains under compression, as when standing on the floor. A lift by the armpits results in most of the body experiencing extension forces, with only the upper spine and neck supporting compressive forces. These changes in the distribution of compressive and extension forces challenge the lifted dancer to maintain body placement and line that are aesthetically pleasing.

One of the most valuable concepts in the application of physical principles of dance involves linear and rotational momentum. (The latter will be discussed in appendix B.) Momentum can be thought of as a quantity of motion, involving both the mass of a body and its velocity. The magnitude of linear momentum is just the product of mass and velocity, and its direction is the direction of the velocity. It can be shown that momentum is a conserved quantity—that is, the momentum of a system does not change if there are no total forces acting on it, even if there are interactions or changes within the system. Suppose one person moving horizontally collides with another. If friction is ignored, the total momentum of the two after the collision will equal the total momentum of the two before, which will be just the momentum of the first person if the second was initially at rest. An example of this phenomenon occurs with a partnered running catch. If a woman has a certain linear momentum while running to her standing partner and then jumps to be caught by him, their combined momentum just after the catch will equal her momentum before. The "catcher" then can be seen to decelerate their combined mass by exerting a force against the floor to slow their forward motion.

A single body may also be considered as a "system" composed of many parts. If the body is at rest with no outside forces acting on it, and one part is displaced to one side, the rest of the body will recoil in the opposite direction, maintaining a zero total momentum of the system (and a zero velocity of the center of gravity).

Appendix B
Rotational Mechanics

A SET OF LAWS and kinematic equations may be developed for rotational motion that are quite analogous to those described for linear motion in appendix A. Let A be the rotational displacement (or angle of change in rotational orientation) in degrees of arc; ω (Greek lowercase omega), the rotational velocity (or rate of turn or turning speed) in degrees per second; α (Greek lowercase alpha), the rotational acceleration (or the rate at which the turning speed changes); and t, the time. Then

$$A = \omega t,$$
$$\omega_2 - \omega_1 = \alpha t,$$
$$\omega_2^2 - \omega_1^2 = 2\alpha A, \ and$$
$$A = \left(\frac{1}{2}\right)\alpha t^2.$$

Recall the dancer in appendix A who was moving downstage at a velocity of 5 feet per second. A rotational analogue would be a dancer turning at a rate of, let's say, one revolution ($360°$ turn) every 2 seconds, for a rotational velocity of $180°$ per second. If 2 seconds later she is rotating at a rate of a full revolution every second, or 360° per second, the rotational acceleration would be the difference in those rotational velocities divided by 2 seconds (the time interval during which the rotational velocity changed), or 90° per second per second. The other two equations follow by analogy with their linear counterparts in the same way.

The rotational analogue of Newton's laws of linear motion may be expressed by substituting variables appropriate for the description of rotational motion for the corresponding linear quantities, giving rise to a system of equations for rotational dynamics. In this case position, velocity, and acceleration are replaced by their rotational counterparts; force is replaced by "torque," which may be thought of as a twisting force; and mass is replaced by "rotational inertia," which is a measure of a body's inertial resistance to a change in rotational motion. (See table B.1 at the end of the chapter.)

A torque arises from a force acting on a body along a line displaced from the body's center of gravity. For convenience we will consider torques that produce no linear acceleration; in that case a torque is produced by a force "couple," which is two equal and opposite forces acting on a body, for which the lines of action of the forces are not coincident, but are parallel with some distance d between them, as in the diagram in figure B.1. The magnitude of the torque is given by the product of the force and the separation distance d, called the "moment arm."

One example of a force couple is the opposite forces exerted by the two separated feet when a dancer begins a *pirouette*. Another is the opposite tangential forces exerted by the two hands of a partner when initiating the supported *fouetté pirouette* described in chapter 7. If the right hand pulls back and the left hand

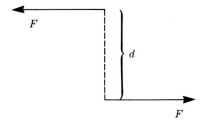

FIGURE B.1. A force couple. The two forces have equal magnitudes F.

pushes forward at the waist of the partnered dancer, she will be given a rotational acceleration toward the right, or clockwise viewed from above.

The rotational inertia depends on the mass of a body *and its distribution relative to the axis of rotation.* A body of given mass will have a larger rotational inertia if the mass is far from the axis of rotation than if it is close. An *arabesque* or *à la seconde* position, as shown in figure B.2, has a larger rotational inertia than a *retiré* or *passé* position.

The rotational analogue of Newton's second law can be simply stated:

$$T = Fd = I\alpha,$$

where T is the torque, whose magnitude is given by the product of the force and the separation distance for a force couple; I is the rotational inertia; and α is the rotational acceleration. Clearly, if the torque is zero, there is no rotational acceleration, and the rotational velocity is constant (perhaps zero). If there *is* a torque, its magnitude is large if either the force is large or the separation between the parallel lines of action of the forces is large. For instance, a *pirouette* from fifth position, for which the separation of the forces is small, is more difficult to initiate than a *pirouette* from fourth position, with the feet separated. For a given torque, the rotational velocity will increase rapidly if I is small, which will be true if the body's mass is compacted close to the axis of rotation. Chapter 7 deals with torques and force couples as they apply to the initiation of supported *pirouettes.*

A powerful concept for dance analysis involves rotational momentum. Analogous to linear momentum, rotational momentum L is given by the product of the rotational inertia I and rotational velocity. Thus

$$L = I\omega.$$

If there are no torques on a body the rotational momentum L is a constant. But now, unlike the case of linear momentum in which the mass is constant, both the rotational inertia and the rotational velocity can change. This fact has broad implica-

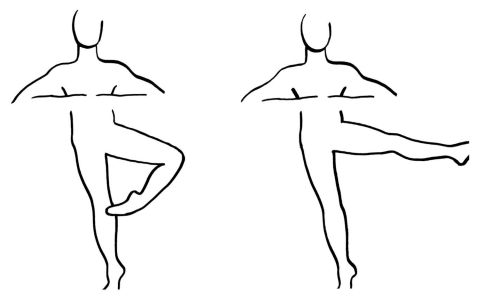

FIGURE B.2. The two body configurations shown here have different values of rotational inertia (or "moment of inertia"), which is greater when the body is extended than when it is close to the axis of rotation.

tions. For instance, even if there are no torques to change a dancer's rotational momentum around a vertical axis, the rotational velocity can still be changed by causing a change in the distribution of mass relative to the axis of rotation. A spinning ice skater increases the rate of turn by bringing the arms and legs closer to the axis. Or a dancer doing a *grande pirouette* speeds up noticeably when the arms and legs are brought from an extended position into a normal *pirouette* position. In linear motion, since it is impossible to change one's mass or weight suddenly, the linear velocity cannot be changed without some force being exerted on the body to change its linear momentum.

If there *is* a torque, there will generally be a rotational acceleration. But because both the rotational inertia and the rotational velocity can change, the dynamic equation relating torque to change in rotational motion is actually a little more subtle than that given earlier. The more general relationship is that *the torque is equal to the rate of change of rotational momentum.* In the special case of constant rotational inertia, this relationship reduces to

Table B.1 Analogous linear and rotational quantities for kinematics and dynamics in one dimension

Quantity	Linear	Rotational
Time	t	t
Position	s	A
Velocity	v	ω
Acceleration	a	α
Cause of change in motion	Force (F)	Torque (T)
Inertia	Mass (m)	Rotational inertia (I)
Momentum	p	L

$$T = I\alpha,$$

as stated before. But now one can see that, for a given torque, the rotational acceleration will be small if I is large. This is desirable if one wants to acquire a significant rotational momentum without accelerating too rapidly away from the initial position from which the accelerating torque is exerted. After the rotational momentum is acquired, the rotational inertia can be decreased, thus allowing the rotational velocity to increase. This process is particularly noticeable in a *pirouette en dedans* with *degagé seconde*, in which the back push-off foot swings out while the body turns very little, then moves in to *pirouette* position as the body turns more rapidly.

Note that the "rotations" described here may involve rotations not only of the body as a whole but of its individual parts. For instance, when the legs move in a scissors-like motion back and forth ("beats" in dance), they are actually rotating around an axis at the hip joint. The "beats" of the legs moving apart and then back together are rotational oscillations, requiring rotational accelerations outward and then inward. For these accelerations, muscles around the hip joint exert forces along lines displaced from the center of rotation in the joint, producing the required torques.

Appendix C
Anatomical Data for Dancers

QUANTIFYING BODY segment lengths and masses for dancers is no easy task. Lengths of thighs, forearms, and other body parts can be measured directly, but determining their masses and quantifying their shapes are far more challenging tasks. For many years information from the weighing of dismembered cadavers was sometimes used. Other techniques have been less precise but more applicable to typical participants in sports and dance.

About thirty years ago Stanley Plagenhoef[1] summarized the work of several investigators who determined, by measurement or modeling, body segment masses and lengths. The data include averages for six female college-age gymnasts (presumed to be more representative of dancers than the general female population) and for thirty-five college-age men. This information is summarized in table c.1.

More recent data, using modern techniques of measurement, have been reported by Zatsiorsky et al.[2] and evaluated and interpreted by Paolo de Leva from

1. S. Plagenhoef, *Patterns of Human Motion* (Englewood Cliffs, N.J.: Prentice-Hall, 1971), chapter 3; S. Plagenhoef, after W. T. Dempster, "Space Requirements of the Seated Operator," WADC Technical Report: 55–159, 1955.; S. Plagenhoef, after K. Kjeldsen, "Body Segment Weights of College Women" (master's thesis, University of Massachusetts, 1969).
2. V. M. Zatsiorsky, V. N. Seluyanov, and L. G. Chugunova, "Methods of Determining

Table C.1 Weights (as percentage of total body weight) and lengths (as percentage of total body height) of body segments for six female college-age gymnasts and thirty-five college-age men (after Plagenhoef).

Body Segment	Men		Women	
	Weight	Length	Weight	Length
Trunk	48.3	30.0	50.8	30.0
Head	7.1	—	9.4	—
Thigh	10.5	23.2	8.3	24.7
Shank	4.5	24.7	5.5	25.6
Foot	1.5	—	1.2	—
Upper arm	3.3	17.2	2.7	19.3
Forearm	1.9	15.7	1.6	16.6
Hand	0.6	—	0.5	—

the Istituto Superiore di Educazione Fisica di Roma, Italy, and Indiana University Kinesiology Department (Bloomington, Indiana). The test group of females for these data were nine college athletes in track and field and diving. The data include not only masses and lengths of body segments but carefully defined end points for the segments and locations of their centers of gravity. The test group, however, is not as applicable to the dance population, since the average of the females' total height was about 4 percent greater and body weight 32 percent greater than the data used here for a slender female dancer. Data for male athletes differed only slightly from those reported by Plagenhoef. So data summarized in *The Physics of Dance* in 1984 still seem to be the most viable for these purposes.

Mass-Inertial Characteristics of Human Body Segments," in G. G. Chernyi, and S. A. Regirer, eds., *Contemporary Problems of Biomechanics*, pp. 272–91 (Boca Raton, Fla.: CRC Press, 1990).

Appendix D
Rotational Inertia for Some
Body Configurations

THERE ARE TWO ways in which rotational inertia is important in analyzing the dynamics of rotational motion. First, for a given torque, the rotational inertia determines the change of rotational momentum that occurs in a particular time interval. Second, if the torque is negligible, the rotational momentum is constant, and the rotational velocity is related to the rotational inertia, which can be changed by varying the body configuration. For example, a change in body position that causes the rotational inertia to double will decrease the rotational velocity by one-half. (See appendix B for a basic discussion of rotational motion.)

Several analyses require knowing the rotational inertia of the body or parts of the body in various positions, around various rotation axes. Those calculations can be simplified by first considering some simple geometrical shapes. A point mass of mass M revolving on the end of a string a distance R from the center (or axis) of rotation will have a rotational inertia $I = MR^2$. Geometrical shapes in which the mass is distributed through the volume of the object may be treated as a collection of point masses, each having some small mass and an associated distance from the rotation axis. Table D.1 gives some representative values of rotational inertia for simple geometrical shapes.

One rotational inertia we will need is that of a rigid leg oscillating around a horizontal axis through the hip joint. A rough calculation will give a good idea of the magnitude of this rotational inertia for a male of height 6 ft 1/2 in (about 1.84 m) and weight 159 lb (72 kg). (These figures roughly fit Sean Lavery, who is the model for the movements described in chapter 9.) The total rotational inertia of the leg will be made up of contributions from the thigh, shank, and foot. Data from appendix C will be used, along with equations for moments of inertia of uniform masses. The thigh is assumed to be a uniform rod oscillating around one end. The shank is a uniform rod oscillating around an axis $l_1 + (1/2)l_2$ from its center of gravity. We will assume the foot to be a point mass a distance $l_1 + l_2$ from the axis through the hip. (The subscripts 1, 2, and 3 refer to the thigh, shank, and foot, respectively.) The total rotational inertia is then

$$I = \tfrac{1}{3}m_1 l_1{}^2 + m_2\left\{\tfrac{1}{12}l_2{}^2 + [l_1 + \tfrac{1}{2}l_2]^2\right\} + m_3(l_1 + l_2)^2.$$

Using the data for Sean, the tall dancer, and "Shorty" of chapter 9 (Sean is 15 percent larger than Shorty in all linear dimensions), the magnitudes of moments of inertia for the oscillating leg are

Table D.1 Rotational inertia values for some simple geometrical shapes

Shape	Axis	Rotational Inertia
Rod, length L {	Middle	$(1/12)ML^2$
	One end	$(1/3)ML^2$
	Dist. D beyond one end	$M\left[\tfrac{1}{12}L^2 + (D + \tfrac{1}{2}L)^2\right]$
Cylinder, radius R, length L	Center axis	$(1/2)MR^2$
	Parallel edge	$(3/2)MR^2$
Sphere, radius R	Center	$(2/5)MR^2$
Circular ring, radius R	Edge, perpendicular to plane	$2MR^2$

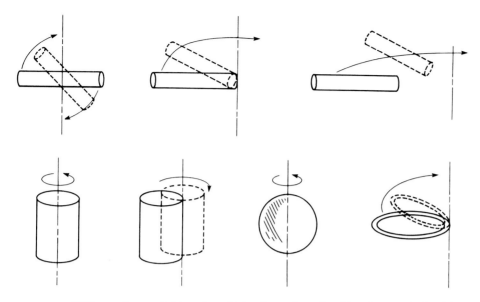

$$I = 2.75 \; kg\text{–}m^2 \; \textit{for Sean, and}$$
$$I = 1.37 \; kg\text{–}m^2 \; \textit{for Shorty.}$$

Now consider another important body configuration: the normal *pirouette* position. This will be idealized as a vertical body with the gesture leg in *retiré* (foot at the opposite knee), and the arms making a horizontal circle in front of the body. These calculations will be somewhat crude, but it is important to recognize two aspects of this analysis. First, bodies differ significantly, so accuracy in the calculations is not useful. Second, the purpose here will be to demonstrate some relative magnitudes of rotational inertia, which lead to interesting characteristics of the motions involved, rather than to develop accurate quantitative analyses.

Let us take as our example a female of height 1.6 m (5 ft 3 in) and mass 44 kg (97 lb). Assume the head and trunk form a uniform cylinder of effective radius 12 cm, rotating around its vertical axis of symmetry along with the supporting leg, having an effective average radius of 4 cm. These estimates of radius are crude, and take into account the fact that mass far from the axis is weighted more heavily than mass close to the axis. The hips, for instance, contribute a significant fraction of the rotational inertia of the rotating body because they are generally larger in women than other parts of the body.

Adding the different contributions to the total rotational inertia, and using the data of appendix C for our sample female, the rotational inertia for this symmetric part of the body is

$$I_1 = \left(\tfrac{1}{2}\right) mr^2 = 0.20 \text{ kg–m}^2,$$

The gesture leg forms an equilateral triangle to the side of the axis of rotation. Its contribution to the total I is

$$I_2 = \tfrac{1}{3}(m_1 + m_2)\,(l\cos 30°)^2 = 0.25 \text{ kg–m}^2,$$

where m_1 and m_2 are the masses of the thigh and shank, respectively. The arms form a circle of radius about 20 cm, with the axis through one edge. Their contribution to the total rotational inertia is

$$I_3 = 2m_a r^2 = 0.17 \text{ kg–m}^2,$$

where m_a is the total mass of the arms. The total rotational inertia of a body rotating in *pirouette* position is thus

$$I = 0.62 \text{ kg–m}^2.$$

Now, for the purpose of analyzing the *fouetté* turn, consider the rotational inertia of the gesture leg alone as it is extended horizontally to the front and rotates to the side. This is effectively the same physical rotation as the oscillating leg analyzed earlier. The total I for our model female is

$$I_1 = 2.55 \text{ kg–m}^2.$$

In appendix I a solo *fouetté* turn is analyzed numerically; in appendix J a supported *fouetté* turn, or whip turn, is analyzed. These derived values of rotational inertia will be used in those analyses.

Appendix E
Acceleration Away from Balance

I MAGINE THE BODY as an idealized "stick" of length L somewhat heavier at the upper end than the lower. This stick can be balanced vertically on the floor. If it is displaced from the vertical by a small initial angle θ_o, it will start toppling, and the angle θ will increase at an accelerating rate.

The force of gravity acts on the center of gravity and thus exerts a torque around the point of support whenever the stick is displaced from the vertical. (See figure E.1.) The equation relating the rotational acceleration α away from the vertical and the torque T due to gravity is

$$T = mgR_c \, sin \, \theta = I\alpha = mR_g^2\alpha,$$

where m is the mass of the body, g is the acceleration due to gravity, R_c is the distance from the point of support to the center of gravity, I is the rotational inertia of the body toppling around an axis through the point of support, R_g is the radius of gyration (defined as $\sqrt{I/m}$), and α is the toppling rotational acceleration. If the angle is small, $sin \, \theta$ may be replaced by θ with very little error. The resulting simple differential equation has as a solution, taking into account the initial conditions,

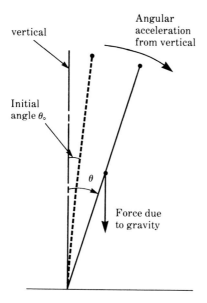

vertical

Angular
acceleration
from vertical

Initial
angle θ_o

θ

Force due
to gravity

FIGURE E.1. The toppling of a vertical rod.

$$\theta = \theta_o \cosh \left[\sqrt{gR_c/R_g^2} \right] t,$$

where $\cosh K t$ represents a hyperbolic cosine function of time t with constant coefficient K, where K has the value $\sqrt{gR_c/R_g^2}$.

For a uniform stick of length 5 ft 10 in (or 1.78 m), the center of mass would be at the midpoint, so $R_c = 0.89$ m; R_g would be 1.03 m. Assuming the body is more massive at the upper end, let us increase each of these quantities arbitrarily by 15 percent. Thus $R_c = 1.02$ m and $R_g = 1.18$ m, and the coefficient of t in the above equation has the numerical value 2.7/s.

Note that this coefficient is greater for a small person, so that the acceleration away from vertical is, as one would expect, more rapid than for a larger person.

Table E.1 shows the angle of displacement from the vertical in degrees as it varies with time for a few initial angles of displacement, for a 5 ft 10 in dancer and one 15 percent smaller (just under 5 ft). Note how rapidly the angle increases, doubling about every 1/4 s after the early acceleration from vertical. Even for relatively small initial angles, the toppling is very rapid after a time of only a second or so.

Table E.1 Increase of angle of displacement from the vertical for tall and short toppling dancers, for different initial angles of displacement

Height	Time (seconds)	Angle from Vertical (degrees)			
	Start	0.5	1.0	2.0	4.0
	0.5	1.0	2.1	4.1	8.2
5 ft 10 in	1.0	3.7	7.5	15	30
	1.5	14	29	57	>60
	2.0	55	>60	>60	>60
	Start	0.5	1.0	2.0	4.0
	0.5	1.1	2.3	4.5	9.0
5 ft 0 in	1.0	4.6	9.1	18	36
	1.5	20	39	>60	>60
	2.0	>60	>60	>60	>60

The challenge to dancers is to ensure that they are initially as close as possible to the balance condition, and that they carry out the appropriate motions to adjust balance very quickly, before the departure from vertical is too large to correct.

Appendix F
Off-Balance *Pirouettes*

SUPPOSE A DANCER is off balance while performing a *pirouette*. What action is necessary in order for the dancer to regain balance?

The choice of the appropriate technique of analysis depends on the magnitude of the spinning rotational momentum. If this L is not very large, then the effects of rotation can be ignored, and the process of restoring balance can be analyzed as if the dancer were not rotating but just poised above the supporting point at the floor; that analysis is described in chapter 2. If the spinning rotational momentum *is* large, then the motion and its analysis are more complicated. The turning, off-balance dancer would have to be treated like a spinning top (or gyroscope), with the possibility of precession of the rotation axis (the circling of the axis of a top on a path like an inverted cone).

In order to make a judgment about the magnitude of the spinning rotational momentum, that L must be compared with the toppling rotational momentum produced by the torque due to gravity acting on the unbalanced body. This torque is given in appendix E as

$$T = mgR_c \, sin \, \theta,$$

where m is the mass of the body, g is the acceleration due to gravity, R_c is the height to the center of gravity, and θ is the angle of lean of the body from the vertical. In appendix B we saw that torque equals the rate of change of rotational momentum, so that a change in rotational momentum occurring in a time Δt is given by

$$\Delta L = (mgR_c \sin \theta) \Delta t.$$

If the body spins through many revolutions while the ΔL causes a small change in direction of the almost-vertical spinning L associated with the spinning, then precession results, and the dancer's balance is essentially maintained without adjustments having to be made.

Let us estimate some numerical values of the quantities involved. Assume a female dancer of mass 50 kg (110 lb) and height 1.7 m (5 ft 7 in) is rotating in normal *pirouette* position at a rotational velocity of two revolutions per second, or 12.6 rad/s. As shown in appendix D, her rotational inertia will be about 0.7 kg–m². Her rotational momentum of spin will then be

$$L = I\omega = (0.7) (12.6) = 8.8 \text{ kg–m}^2\text{/s}.$$

Now consider the toppling. The dancer's center of gravity is about 1.0 m above the floor. Suppose the angle of displacement from the vertical is 2°. (Ignoring the rotating motion, that angle would increase to about 4° after 1/2 s.) The torque is then 17 kg-m /s², giving rise to a change of rotational momentum of 8.5 kg–m²/s in the 1/2 s it takes to complete one revolution of the *pirouette*.

It appears that the condition for precession mentioned earlier is *not* met once the angle from the vertical exceeds a degree or two. That is, the change in rotational momentum associated with toppling that would occur in the time it takes for several rotations is not small compared to the spin rotational momentum, and the rotation can be ignored. Of course, if the angle of displacement is significantly smaller than a degree or two, or if the turn rate is greater, the rotation *would* be important. In that case, the rotation would actually *help* a dancer maintain balance, for the same reason a top topples more slowly when spinning than when not spinning. So one might expect that if the turning body is very close to balance initially, the effort needed to keep it there is small. But once the departure from vertical exceeds a couple of degrees, then the toppling will occur as if the body is not rotating. Ice skaters are aware of this situation, and their turn rate is fast enough that they probably do depend on the spinning-top effect to stay balanced.

Appendix G
Arabesque Turn Analysis

O NE POTENTIAL problem in performing an *arabesque* turn is the "drooping-leg syndrome." The gesture leg, which is supposed to be extended roughly horizontally to the rear, tends to descend during the turn because of the downward pull of gravity. The rotational inertia of the rotating body decreases as the leg's mass is brought down and therefore closer to the axis of rotation, which allows the rotational velocity to increase. The more rapid rotation produces an increase in the centrifugal force, which tends to throw the gesture leg back out to the rear, giving rise to an up and down oscillation of the leg.

This problem was described in chapter 4, and the result of a detailed analysis was mentioned indicating that the period of oscillation of the leg can be close to the period of rotation, making the problem particularly insidious. The more detailed analysis will now be described.

The body is assumed to consist of three main body parts, as shown in the diagram of figure G.1. The effect of the arms in contributing to the rotational inertia will be ignored because they are so light, and the contribution of the supporting leg

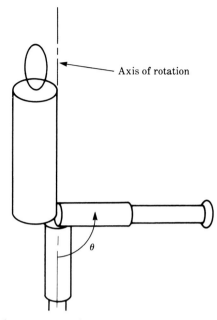

Axis of rotation

θ

FIGURE G.1. Idealized body model for the *arabesque* turn analysis.

will be ignored because its mass is concentrated so close to the axis of rotation. The axis of rotation will be assumed to be vertical, oriented along the edge of the cylindrical torso and head. We will assume a female of height 5 ft 3 in (1.60 m), weight 97 lb (44 kg), and effective radius of the torso 12 cm. The other masses and body segment lengths are taken from appendix C.

The total rotational inertia of a cylinder rotating around an axis along its edge is

$$I_b = \left(\frac{3}{2}\right) M_b r^2 = 0.66 \text{ kg–m}^2.$$

The rotational inertia of the gesture leg making an angle θ with the vertical is

$$I_1 = I_0 \sin^2 \theta,$$

where $I_0 = 1.44$ kg–m², from a calculation similar to that found in appendix D.

The effect of the centrifugal force on the leg can be treated as a torque around a horizontal axis through the hip, tending to increase the angle θ. This torque is proportional to the square of the rotational velocity ω and has a value (after integrating over the length of the leg and substituting assumed masses and lengths)

$$T_1 = (1.44 \text{ kg--m}^2)\, \omega^2 \sin\theta \cos\theta.$$

The torque tending to decrease θ (lower the leg) is due to gravity acting on the center of gravity of the leg and is found to be

$$T_2 = (25.5 \text{ kg--m}^2/\text{s}^2) \sin\theta.$$

The total torque on the leg tending to increase its angle with the vertical is thus, in standard meter-kilogram-second units,

$$T = 1.44\, \omega^2 \sin\theta \cos\theta - 25.5 \sin\theta.$$

The rotational momentum of the rotating body will be assumed constant (no accelerating or retarding torques between the supporting foot and the floor). What is this rotational momentum? Let us choose a rotation rate of 0.8 revolutions per second, with the leg at the equilibrium angle for that rotation rate, such that the dancer is exerting no torque in the hip to support the leg. (This is artificial, since most dancers *will* exert a torque to help support the leg. That torque will be taken into account later as a perturbing factor in the simpler analysis.)

The equilibrium angle can be found by setting the total torque in the above equation to zero and finding the θ that corresponds to the assumed value of ω. The result is $\theta_o = 45°$. Now with that θ the total rotational inertia can be found from the first equation, and the rotational momentum is

$$L = 6.95 \text{ kg--m/s}.$$

If this rotational momentum is a constant even when the angle θ and the rotation rate change, we can use that fact to eliminate ω from the equation for total torque. The rotational velocity is given by

$$\omega = L/I = \frac{6.95}{I_b + I_0 \sin^2\theta} = \frac{4.84}{0.46 + \sin^2\theta}$$

Now we can construct an expression for the torque tending to change the leg angle θ in terms of just one variable, θ. Since torque is the product of the rotational inertia of the leg around the horizontal hip axis and the rotational acceleration α of the leg around that axis, we have a final expression

$$1.44\,\alpha = 1.44 \left[\frac{4.84}{0.46 + \sin^2\theta} \right]^2 \sin\theta \cos\theta - 25.5 \sin\theta.$$

This is a nontrivial differential equation, which can be solved by assuming the change of θ from θ_o is small. The numerical result of this solution is that the frequency of oscillation is about 1.1 cycles per second. This frequency is close enough to the turn rate of 0.8 revolutions per second that, with the significant uncertainties in the analysis, the two may be equal, giving rise to a "resonance" in which the leg undergoes one up-down-up oscillation while the body turns one complete turn. There is undoubtedly a mental reinforcement for an oscillation that involves a slowing of the body's rotation each time the dancer is facing the side, with the arabesque line facing the audience. This reinforcement would be particularly strong if the head is also spotting to that direction once each revolution.

Now suppose that our cavalier assumption about the lack of torque from the hip is reconsidered. Suppose the hip exerts a constant lifting torque such that the equilibrium angle of the leg is increased to 75° from the vertical. The torque necessary to accomplish that more nearly horizontal *arabesque* position can be calculated and has a numerical value of

$$T_H = 15.6 \text{ kg–m}^2/\text{s}^2 \ .$$

The total constant rotational momentum is greater in this case, since the leg is extended farther from the axis of rotation. The relationship between the rotational acceleration of the leg around the hip joint and the angle θ must take into account the additional hip torque. A solution of the revised equation produces the result that the oscillation frequency is 0.9 cycles per second, a bit slower than for oscillations around the lower angle of 45°. In fact, this oscillation frequency is even closer to the frequency of rotation, implying an even closer coupling between the rotation and the oscillating leg.

Again the result is important because the natural tendency to slow the turn, or pause, after each revolution is enhanced by the "drooping-leg syndrome," in which the leg is high and the rotation slow, then the leg descends, speeding the turn, then rises again after about one revolution to slow the turn when the body again is facing the original direction. The fact that the movement is performed without the culprit leg in sight of the dancer makes it difficult to correct this fault, which has such a negative effect on the aesthetic line of the *arabesque* position during the turn.

How does a dancer benefit from this understanding? Knowing that the leg will tend to droop down and increase the speed of the turn, the dancer consciously exerts enough torque in the hip so that when the leg reaches its highest angle, it stays there. The vertical oscillation of the leg is then diminished. But the dancer also realizes that the average rate of turn is slower because the leg resides farther from the rotation axis throughout the turn.

Appendix H
Quantitative Analysis of
the *Grande Pirouette*

THE GRANDE PIROUETTE is a turn on one supporting leg with the gesture leg extended horizontally to the side (second position *en l'air*). A detailed analysis is quite involved, even when several simplifying assumptions are made. The results of the analysis will be outlined here.

Assume the body can be represented by two legs, each of mass m and length l (and negligible thickness), plus the remainder of the body, of mass M, effective length L, symmetric around the longitudinal axis. The legs consist of a thigh of length $(1/2)l$ and mass $(2/3)m$, and a shank and foot of length $(1/2)l$ and mass $(1/3)m$. (These assumptions are within a few percent of data on human bodies given by Plagenhoef and described in appendix C.) Leg number 1, the supporting leg, makes an angle θ with the vertical; leg number 2, the gesture leg, is horizontal; the remainder of the body is effectively vertical. (See figure H.1.)

Now the question is whether there is a difference in the angle θ for static equilibrium and for the case where the body is rotating about the vertical axis.

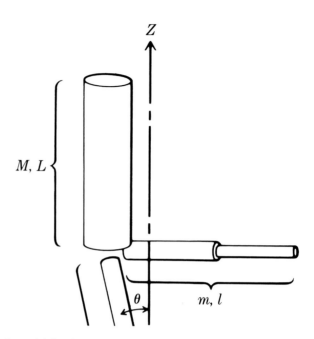

FIGURE H.1. Idealized body model for the *grande pirouette* analysis.

Static Equilibrium

The condition for static equilibrium is that the torques acting on the body around its pivot (the supporting foot on the floor) must add to zero. These torques are due to gravity acting downward on the center of gravity of each of the body segments. Let us first find the position of the center of gravity for each of the three segments in the idealized model of the body. Simple calculations show that the center of gravity of the idealized leg is 7/12 of the total leg length from the foot end, or 5/12 of the leg length from the hip. The center of gravity of the remainder of the body will be assumed to be in the center of the cylinder, since only its horizontal position is important for the analysis.

The total torque acting in a clockwise direction around the supporting foot is now given by

$$T = -mgl\left(\frac{7}{12}\sin\theta\right) - Mgl\sin\theta + mgl\left(\frac{5}{12} - \sin\theta\right).$$

For static equilibrium, that total torque must be zero. Solving the equation for θ produces the result

$$\theta = 4.4°.$$

Dynamic Equilibrium

Assume the axis of rotation is vertical. For an object that is symmetric around that vertical axis, that axis would be a "principal axis," and the rotational momentum could also be considered to have only a vertical component. But since the body in *grande pirouette* position is clearly not symmetric, the vector representing the rotational momentum will not be vertical. (In physics terms, the inertia tensor relating rotational velocity to rotational momentum will have nonzero off-diagonal elements.)

Since the rotational momentum is not vertical, it must precess around the vertical axis as the body rotates, forming a cone with the apex at the supporting point. But the rotational momentum can change only if there is a torque acting on the body. Since the only source of torque for a freely rotating body is gravitational force, we conclude that the condition derived for static balance must not be met, so that in fact there *is* a net torque just sufficient to produce the rate of change of rotational momentum giving rise to the precession.

In order to find the nonvertical component of the rotational momentum, the reader familiar with a more advanced level of physics will recognize that it is necessary to find the elements of the inertia tensor for each of the rotating body segments. It can be shown that the magnitude of torque needed is

$$T' = \omega^2 I_{xz},$$

where I_{xz} is the *xz* element of the inertia tensor. That torque is then equated to the torque equation used for static equilibrium, recognizing that now the torque will not be zero, and the angle will not be 4.4°. The result of the calculation is that the angle is in fact about 3.5° for a rotation rate of one revolution per second. The effect will of course be stronger for a faster turn.

Thus, when the body is rotating, a small correction must be made in the angle the supporting leg makes with the vertical, shifting the body toward the extended gesture leg. That is, the total-body center of gravity, which is directly over the supporting point for static equilibrium, must be displaced when rotating to a location slightly to the right of the vertical axis through the supporting point in figure H.1. As the turn slows, the effect diminishes, and the center of gravity must be shifted back toward the vertical line through the supporting foot.

Appendix I
Quantitative Analysis of
the *Fouetté* Turn

THE FOUETTÉ TURN is described in chapter 4. The rotational inertia values necessary for analyzing this movement quantitatively were calculated in appendix D for a female dancer of height 1.6 m (5 ft 3 in) and mass 44 kg (97 lb).

Assume the torque between the supporting foot and the floor is zero, so the body will coast in its rotating motion with constant rotational momentum. The mechanical process in the *fouetté* turn involves a transfer of rotational momentum between the whole rotating body during the turn and the gesture leg alone when the rest of the body is temporarily stationary *en face*. This constant rotational momentum can be expressed as

$$L = I_b \omega_b = I_l \omega_l,$$

where I_b and ω_b are the rotational inertia and rotational velocity of the whole body in *pirouette* position, and I_l and ω_l are those quantities for the extended leg alone. Suppose ω_b is about 2.0 revolutions per second, or 12.6 rad/s during the turning phase. Then, since the rotational momentum is the same, the turn rate when only the leg is rotating can be found, using the rotational inertia from appendix D:

$$L = (0.62) (12.6) = (2.55) (\omega_l), \text{ and}$$
$$\omega_l = 3.05 \text{ rad/s} = 0.49 \text{ rev/s}.$$

Thus the leg alone will rotate around the vertical body axis at a rate of about 1/2 revolution per second, which means that the 1/4 revolution needed to move the leg from front to side will occupy about 1/2 s.

Given the approximations used in the model for this *fouetté* turn, the time required to complete each turning phase of the movement (1/2 second at a 2 revolution per second rate) is equal to the time during which most of the body is stationary while the gesture leg rotates through its quarter turn from front to side.

Note that if the arm on the same side of the body as the moving leg rotates with the leg from front to side, as is often the case when *fouetté* turns are performed, the effective rotational inertia for that phase of the movement is greater. The result is that the arm and leg will rotate more slowly while the rest of the body is temporarily at rest. That slower rotation could occupy more time than the 1/2 s calculated, *or*, more likely, the arm and leg could rotate for the same length of time but through an angle smaller than 90° before returning to the *pirouette* position.

Appendix J
Quantitative Analysis of the
Supported *Fouetté* Turn

THE SUPPORTED FOUETTÉ turn is discussed in chapter 7 and shown in the photographs in figure 7.2. This is a movement in which, for a turn to the right, the woman starts facing the audience *en pointe* on her left supporting leg, with her right leg extended a little to the left of directly in front of her. Her partner is behind her, hands on her waist, prepared to exert a forward force with his left hand and a backward force with his right in order to initiate the turn. When he starts to exert those forces, rather than allow herself to be turned immediately, she rotates her right leg from front to side, thereby absorbing the rotational momentum generated by her partner's forces (torque) on her. After the right leg reaches the side, she brings it in to the *pirouette* position, thus transferring the rotational momentum gained by the leg to the body as a whole. She then rotates as in a normal *pirouette*.

What is gained by performing the supported *pirouette* in this way? Why doesn't she just allow her body to start rotating *as* her partner exerts the forces with his hands at her waist? Some quantitative calculations will demonstrate the benefit of the proper technique for the supported *fouetté* by providing a comparison of the magnitudes of rotational velocity resulting from the two techniques.

We will draw on the results derived in appendixes D and I for the magnitudes of rotational inertia for a female ballet dancer's body. For the dancer of height 5 ft 3 in weighing 97 lb, the rotational inertia for the extended leg alone (in the metric system of units) is $I_l = 2.55$ kg–m^2; for the body as a whole in *pirouette* position (right leg to the side, foot at left knee) it is $I_b = 0.62$ kg–m^2.

Let us first assume that the partner rotates the woman as she remains in a constant *pirouette* position. Suppose the partner exerts a constant torque sufficient to produce a final rotational velocity of 1.0 revolution per second, but that he can exert that torque only through the first 45° of rotation around the vertical axis from the initial position. Using the rotational kinematic equations from appendix B, the time during which he exerts the torque is then 0.25 seconds, and the magnitude of the torque, given by

$$T = I_b \omega / \Delta t,$$

is 15.6 N-m, in metric units.

Now suppose that the man exerts the same torque on the woman's waist, but she starts with the right leg extended horizontally to the front and rotates it around to the side, through an angle of 90° around the vertical axis, as the torque is exerted. Since the leg is the only part of the body rotating, the new final rotational momentum is given by

$$L = I_l \omega_l = T \, \Delta t = T \, (\pi / \omega_l).$$

But when the final rotational momentum of the rotating leg is transferred to the body as a whole,

$$I_b \omega_b = I_l \, \omega_l.$$

Solving these equations for the final rotational velocity of the body after the leg has returned to the *pirouette* position produces the result

$$\omega_b = 2.9 \text{ rev/s},$$

almost three times the rate of rotation produced by the first technique! Thus the *fouetté* technique, in which rotational momentum is stored in the rotating leg while torque is being applied, is significantly more effective in producing a substantial rotation rate than the more direct technique in which the turn is started with the body in the fixed *pirouette* configuration.

Why can the woman gain three times as much rotational speed when the torque exerted by her partner is the same in both cases? The important variable is *the length of time the torque is exerted*. While the leg is rotating from front to side, the woman's partner is exerting the torque for about 0.75 s rather than the 0.25 s in the first case.

Note that there is another advantage to the *fouetté* movement with the gesture leg. The partner is exerting forces on the dancer's waist while she is in an unchanging orientation. It is thus easier for him to maintain her balance than if she were rotating through that 45° angle while he exerts the torque. Also, the torque he can exert while she is in the constant position is probably greater than if her whole body were rotating.

Appendix K
Lean, Don't Slip

THE BALLERINA'S off-balance lean supported by a partner is described in the puzzler at the beginning of chapter 6 and analyzed near the end of the chapter. This predicament and its solution provide a nice opportunity to apply force vector analysis for static equilibrium.

The problem for the dancer is that her feet slip sideways on the floor if there is insufficient friction. Such slipping might occur if the horizontal force exerted by her partner toward the right in figure K.1 is not balanced by a force from the floor directed toward the left. The analysis described in chapter 6 suggests that the partner can overcome that problem by supporting her with a vertical force rather than pushing sideways. We will see here that there is indeed a *range* of ways the partner can exert a force on the dancer that can potentially keep her in static equilibrium, but some ways are more secure than others.

A body is in static equilibrium if the net total force acting on the body is zero *and* the total torque acting around any axis is also zero. In figure K.1, the vertical forces consist of (1) the force of gravity downward of magnitude W (her weight) acting at her center of gravity cg, and (2) the vertical component of the force exerted upward by the floor on her feet. The magnitudes of those two vertical forces must be equal since, in this case, the partner exerts no vertical force on the woman. He

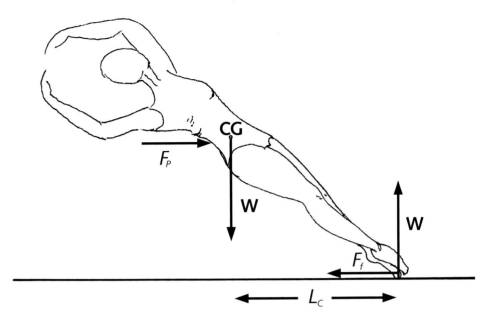

FIGURE K.1. A ballerina held in equilibrium when the partner exerts only a horizontal force on her. Note that there must be sufficient friction to provide the horizontal force at the feet, or else she will slip.

does exert a *horizontal* force on her directed toward the right. That horizontal force F_p must be balanced by the horizontal component F_f of the force exerted on her feet by the floor. That horizontal force cannot be sufficient to balance the partner's force unless there is adequate friction.

Now consider the total torque on the dancer around her point of contact at the floor. That is the simplest axis to consider, since the torques around that axis due to the floor forces are zero. The counterclockwise torque is equal to her weight W times the horizontal distance L_c from her center of gravity *cg* to the contact point. The clockwise torque is the partner's horizontal force F_p times the vertical distance H from his supporting arm to the floor. Since these two torques must add to zero for equilibrium, the resulting equation tells us the magnitude of F_p relative to the total weight W:

$$F_p = W \, (L_c / H).$$

Now the greatest the friction force F_f at the floor can be is the vertical force W times the coefficient of friction k. If k is too small, then the horizontal force at the floor may be smaller than the partner's horizontal force, and she slips! It is clear that the closer she is to vertical, the smaller F_p must be in order to keep her in equilibrium.

Now consider figure K.2, in which the partner exerts only a *vertical* force to support his partner. In this case the torques around the contact point add to zero if the partner's vertical force F_p is related to the weight W by the equation

$$F_p = W \, (L_c / L_p),$$

where L_p is the horizontal distance from the floor contact to the partner's force. In the example shown, L_c is about 3/4 of L_p, so the partner's vertical force is about 3/4 of the ballerina's total weight. In order to make the total force acting on her body zero, the floor must exert a vertical force equal to the proportion of her weight that

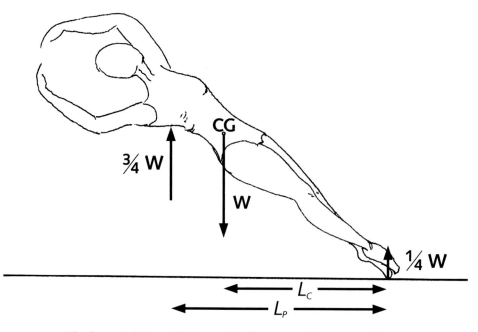

FIGURE K.2. The dancer held in equilibrium with only a vertical force exerted by the partner. Note that there is *no* horizontal force acting on her to make her slip.

is *not* supported by the partner. Note that the fraction of her weight supported by her partner is greater the closer his support is to her center of gravity *cg*.

Note also that in this case there is no horizontal force acting on the woman and therefore *no* tendency for her to slip sideways. But it may be more difficult for her partner to lift vertically with the necessary force rather than push sideways. That, however, is the necessary solution if there is insufficient floor friction!

Figure K.3 shows a way the partner can exert a supporting force F_p on his partner that is intermediate between the two extremes analyzed, for which F_p was entirely horizontal or entirely vertical. The friction force required in this case is not zero, but is less than that required in the first case. Note, however, that the vertical force of the floor on the feet is also less, so that the coefficient of friction may still limit the ability of the partner to keep the ballerina from slipping. The relationship between the magnitude of his force, its location relative to her center of gravity, and the direction of his force may be found through further analysis.

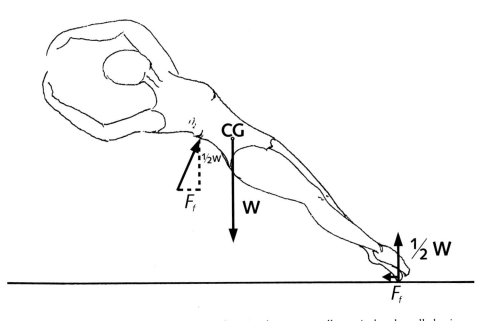

FIGURE K.3. The partner exerts a force in a direction between totally vertical and totally horizontal. Less frictional force is needed in order to avoid the slipping problem, and the angle of the force is more comfortable for the partner than a totally vertical force.

Glossary

Dance Terms

ADAGIO. As in music, a slow tempo: a dance in a slow tempo. Adagios in ballets are often performed by partners. Adagio sections of dance classes are done in a slow tempo.

ALLEGRO. Dancing that is lively and fast, in comparison to adagio.

ARABESQUE. Set pose. In the most common form of *arabesque*, the dancer stands on one leg, with the other leg fully extended to the rear.

ASSEMBLÉ. Literally, "together." A jump from one foot to two feet, ending in fifth position, with the feet "assembling," or coming together, in the air.

ATTITUDE. A pose similar to the *arabesque* but with the raised leg bent. An *attitude en avant* is a similar position but with the bent leg raised to the front.

BARRE. The horizontal bar used by dancers for support and balance in the early part of a ballet class.

BATTEMENT. A beating movement of the legs.

CABRIOLE. A jump in which the legs beat together while in the air. The gesture leg leaves the supporting leg in a kick to any direction; the supporting leg rises to beat against it and then returns to the floor.

CHASSÉ. Literally, "chased." A sliding step.

COUPÉ. A movement in which one foot "cuts" in to the ankle of the supporting leg. In recent use the *coupé* position is a standing position with one foot at the ankle of the other leg.

COURU. Running.

DEGAGÉ. Literally, "disengaged." A small kicking movement in place.

DEMI-FOUETTÉ. A half-turn in which the gesture leg kicks to the front or back, then the body turns through an angle of 180° while leaving the gesture leg pointed in its original direction. The movement may be performed as a jump or with the supporting foot remaining on the floor.

DEMI-POINTE. Standing on the ball of the foot, with the foot pointed except for the toes, which are flat on the floor.

DERRIÈRE. To the rear.

DEVANT. In front.

DEVELOPPÉ. Literally, "developed" or "unfolded." A gradual unfolding of the leg as it rises from the floor and is extended fully in the air. As it is raised, the foot passes the knee of the supporting leg.

EN AVANT. Forward.

EN DEDANS. Inward. Specifically, a turn toward the supporting leg.

EN DEHORS. Outside. Specifically, a turn away from the supporting leg.

EN FACE. Facing front, or toward the audience.

ENTRECHAT. A beating step of elevation in which the dancer leaps straight into the air and crosses the feet a number of times, making a weaving motion in the air. The term *entrechat* is compounded with numerals to indicate the number of movements of the legs. *Entrechat six*, for instance, means six movements of the legs, or three complete crossing/uncrossing cycles.

FIFTH POSITION. A standing position with the feet together and turned out (pointing to the side), heel to toe and toe to heel.

FLIC-FLAC. A turning movement, generally at the barre, in which the working foot makes two inward swipes at the floor during the turn.

FOUETTÉ EN TOURNANT. A turn in which a whipping motion of the free leg propels the dancer around the supporting leg.

GESTURE LEG. The moving leg, opposite to the supporting leg on the floor.

GLISSADE. A gliding movement from fifth position to an open position and back to fifth position.

GRAND(E). Large, as in *grand jeté*, a large jump.

"ILLUSION" TURN. An *en dedans pirouette* in which the body goes through a *penché* position, all but the supporting leg inverted, before recovering back to the upright position.

JETÉ. A jump in which the weight of the body is thrown from one foot to the other.

L'AIR. Aloft, as in *tour en l'air*, a turn in the air.

MANÈGE. A circular series of turns; literally, "a merry-go-round."

PAS DE BOURRÉE. A three-step sequence that reverses the positions of the feet from front to back.

PAS DE DEUX. A dance for two people.

PENCHÉ. Leaning, usually to the front.

PIROUETTE. At least one complete turn of the body on one foot.

PLIÉ. Lowering of the body by bending the knees.

POINTE. "*En pointe*" is dancing on the toes.

QUATRE. Four.

RELEVÉ. The raising of the body onto *pointe* or *demi-pointe*.

RETIRÉ. A standing position in which one foot is at the knee of the supporting leg.

SAUTÉ. Jump.

SECOND POSITION. A standing position facing front with the feet spread apart to the side.

SECONDE. Second, as in *à la seconde*, the leg extended to the side in second position.

TOMBÉ. A lunge to the front, side, or back.

TOUR. A turn.

TOURNANT. Turning.

Physics Terms

ACCELERATION. Rate of change of velocity.

AXIS OF ROTATION. The line around which a body rotates.

CENTER OF GRAVITY. The point at which the gravitational force appears to act on a body as a whole.

FORCE. The magnitude and direction of "push" or "pull." The total of the forces acting on a body determines its rate of change of momentum.

FORCE COUPLE. A pair of equal forces acting in opposite directions along parallel lines. A force couple produces a torque on an object with no net force on it.

INERTIA. Resistance to change in motion. See MASS and ROTATIONAL INERTIA.

LINE OF ACTION. The line along which a force acts, coincident with the direction of the force.

MASS. The inertial resistance to a change in linear motion. A large mass will accelerate less in response to a particular force than a small mass.

MOMENTUM. A quantity of motion, quantitatively equal to the product of the mass and the velocity of a body.

PRECESSION. The circling of the axis of rotation in a cone around the vertical orientation, exemplified by how a spinning top moves as it slows down.

RESONANCE. A phenomenon whereby a periodically changing force has the same frequency as a natural frequency of oscillation of a system, allowing the response of the system to grow to a large magnitude. An example is a person pushing a child in a swing, in which the magnitude of the swinging motion grows because the pushing force has the same timing as the natural timing of the oscillating swing.

ROTATIONAL INERTIA. The inertial resistance to a change in rotational motion. A body with large rotational inertia will undergo a smaller rotational acceleration in response to a particular torque than a body with small rotational inertia. The rotational inertia depends both on the magnitude of mass of a body and on how that mass is distributed relative to the axis of rotation, with a larger rotational inertia associated with mass distributed far from the axis.

ROTATIONAL MOMENTUM. A quantity of rotational motion; the product of the rotational inertia and the rotational velocity.

ROTATIONAL VELOCITY. Rate of change of angular orientation.

ROTATIONAL ACCELERATION. Rate of change of rotational velocity.

SPEED. The magnitude of the velocity, ignoring direction.

TORQUE. "Turning force." The magnitude of torque determines the rate of change of rotational momentum. A torque arising from a force couple will result in *only* rotational acceleration and no linear acceleration. The magnitude of torque for a force couple consisting of two forces F acting in opposite directions and separated by a distance D is just F times D.

VELOCITY. Rate of change of position, with magnitude and direction both specified. The terms "velocity" and "speed" are often used interchangeably in everyday speech.

WEIGHT. The total force of gravity on a body. "Mass" and "weight" are often used interchangeably in everyday speech and in fact are proportional to each other when acted upon by the gravitational force of the earth.

Index